Chocolate *for* Christmas

Also by Maria Robbins

The Dumpling Cookbook
American Corn
Blue-Ribbon Cookies
Blue-Ribbon Pies
Blue-Ribbon Pickles and Preserves
A Cook's Alphabet of Quotations
The Christmas Companion (with Jim Charlton)
A Gardener's Bouquet of Quotations
Cookies for Christmas
Chili!
Baking for Christmas

Chocolate *for* Christmas

Maria Robbins

— ♦♦♦ —

Illustrations by Durell Godfrey

ST. MARTIN'S GRIFFIN ❧ NEW YORK

Library of Congress Cataloging-in-Publication Data

Polushkin, Maria.
    Chocolate for Christmas : 46 of the best recipes for chocolate cookies, cakes, candies, and more, all perfect for holiday gift-giving, decorating, and entertaining / by Maria Robbins.
      p.   cm.
    ISBN 0-312-14566-7
    1. Cookery (Chocolate)   2. Christmas cookery. I. Title.
TX767.C5P65 1996
641.6′374—dc20   96-19275
                                                      CIP

First St. Martin's Griffin Edition: October 1996
10 9 8 7 6 5 4 3 2 1

To Barbara Anderson,
WITH LOVE

Contents

Chocolate for Christmas

Why *Chocolate for Christmas*? Because for many people chocolate, whether in a cookie, brownie, biscotto, cake, or a fine chocolate bonbon, is the one and only luxury and indulgence that is worth the calories. Chocolate is not a ho-hum food. True chocolate lovers are myriad: young and old, plump and thin, and in every corner of the world. They are not just partial to chocolate, they're passionate about it. For chocophiles nothing but irresistible, delectable chocolate provides the same exquisitely rich and satisfying mouth appeal, the soothing and seductive flavor, and the gentle, stimulating lift to the spirits.

I have collected 47 recipes designed to please the most discriminating chocolate lover. You can choose from low-fat but *very* chocolatey biscotti; indulgently rich, intense brownies; sumptuous chocolate truffles; a half dozen chocolate cakes; special Christmas breads; and chocolate cookie classics from America and Europe. As you prepare the recipes from *Chocolate for Christmas,* you may experience the euphoric bliss that comes from the luxury of a home permeated with the intoxicating aroma of baking chocolate. Just try to remember that any gift of chocolate brings happiness to the recipient and a homemade gift of chocolate is even more special.

A CHRISTMAS TIMETABLE

RIGHT AFTER THANKSGIVING

1. Clear out as much space as possible in your freezer, so you have space to freeze breads, cakes, cookies, etc.
2. Make a list of your baking projects and their recipients. Collect the recipes and organize the list in terms of what should be baked first,

to be frozen, aged, or mailed. Be realistic about your time and abilities.

3. Make a shopping list of ingredients and place orders for mail-order items.
4. Check your baking equipment and buy new items as necessary. I always allow myself one special new item at the beginning of each Christmas baking season. This year I bought two nonstick cupcake pans. Here's a quick checklist:
   - parchment paper, waxed paper, foil, plastic wrap, plastic food storage bags in a number of sizes, cellophane, paper doilies, and tissue paper
   - baking pans, cookie sheets, and cooling racks
   - plastic containers with tight-fitting lids in a number of sizes, cookie tins, boxes, and cardboard cake rounds

FIRST WEEK OF DECEMBER

1. Start baking cookies, biscotti, fruitcakes, and items for the freezer.
2. Gather wrapping material and shipping cartons.
3. Gather packing material.
4. Gather labels and package sealing tape.

SECOND WEEK OF DECEMBER

1. Continue baking.
2. Start mailing packages for Christmas delivery.

THIRD WEEK OF DECEMBER

1. Continue baking like crazy.
2. Send packages you didn't send last week.

LAST DAYS BEFORE CHRISTMAS

1. Bake last-minute items for hand-delivered presents.
2. Package and wrap cookies, biscotti, and fruitcakes you baked three weeks ago.
3. Send packages by expensive delivery services because you didn't do it last week.
4. Bake at least one festive yeast bread for Christmas morning.

CHRISTMAS

Relax.

ABOUT CHOCOLATE

If you go to the trouble of baking your own cookies, brownies, biscotti, and cakes or making your own truffles, you should take the trouble to purchase the best quality chocolate you can find. The first thing to do with any chocolate you are about to buy is to check the ingredients. Real chocolate, as opposed to chocolate-flavored products, should contain the following ingredients and nothing more: chocolate, sugar, cocoa butter, lecithin (an emulsifier), and vanilla. Store all chocolate and cocoa, very well wrapped, in a cool, dark place. Do not freeze or refrigerate chocolate.

Properly stored, chocolate will keep for about two years. White chocolate will keep for one year.

TYPES OF CHOCOLATE CALLED FOR IN THIS BOOK:

- **Unsweetened chocolate,** also known as **bitter or baking chocolate,** is the cooled and hardened version of pure chocolate liqueur. It is combined with sugar, and butter, milk, or cream in recipes and it provides an intense chocolate flavor. My first choice is Callebaut unsweetened chocolate, available in Williams-Sonoma stores and catalog. Baker's unsweetened chocolate, available in all supermarkets, is quite suitable.

- **Bittersweet and semisweet chocolate** is chocolate liqueur with the addition of cocoa butter, sugar, and vanilla. Sometimes, but not always, semisweet chocolate is slightly sweeter than bittersweet. They are, however, completely interchangeable. I use Merckens Yucatan classic dark chocolate, available by mail from King Arthur Flour Baker's Catalogue. Other excellent choices are Van Leer bittersweet chocolate, Ghirardelli semisweet chocolate, and Callebaut bittersweet chocolate.

- **Chocolate chips and mini chips** should be made of the finest bittersweet or semisweet chocolate. Always check the ingredients list to make sure that the fat that is used is cocoa butter and not palm oil. Ghirardelli chocolate chips are excellent and can be found on most supermarket shelves.

- **Unsweetened cocoa powder** is made from the hardened chocolate liqueur left after most of the cocoa butter has been removed. It has intense chocolate flavor and is, of course, very low in fat. The cocoa powder called for in this book is Dutch process cocoa powder, which has been treated to reduce its acidity to produce a mellower flavor and darker color. Droste's Dutch process cocoa powder is widely available in supermarkets.

- **White chocolate** is not really chocolate at all. It is made from pure cocoa butter combined with sugar, milk, and vanilla. It has no chocolate liqueur in it at all. Avoid imitation white chocolate, which is made from vegetable oils instead of cocoa butter. Merckens Ivory white chocolate, available by mail from King Arthur Flour Baker's Catalogue, is a good choice.

HOW TO MELT CHOCOLATE AND TOAST NUTS

These two procedures are called for repeatedly throughout the book, so I have outlined them in detail here.

MELTING CHOCOLATE

There are two very strict rules to follow when melting chocolate. Never heat chocolate over direct heat. It will burn much quicker than you can control the heat. Never allow even a drop of water or steam near the melting chocolate. The chocolate will seize up and turn stiff and stubborn. You will have to throw it out and start over. Here are two safe methods for melting chocolate:

Double Boiler

Partially fill the bottom of a double boiler with water and bring to a simmer. Place the coarsely chopped chocolate and any other ingredients to be melted in the top of the double boiler. Set it over the simmering water, but do not let it touch the water. Turn off the heat and stir gently until the chocolate is partially melted. Remove top of pan from double boiler and set on a folded kitchen towel to absorb any moisture. Continue stirring until all the chocolate has melted. If necessary, return water to a simmer and repeat the above procedure.

Microwave

Place the coarsely chopped chocolate and any other ingredients to be melted in a microwave-safe container covered with waxed paper and heat at high power for 20 seconds. Remove the bowl and stir. Repeat until almost completely melted, then stir until the chocolate completes melting from its own heat.

Toasting Nuts

When nuts are called for in these recipes, they are usually nuts that have been lightly toasted to enhance their flavor. All nuts benefit from this treatment, and the process couldn't be simpler. Preheat oven to 350°F. Spread the nuts in a single layer on a baking sheet with sides. Toast for 10 to 15 minutes, until the nuts just begin to color and give off a pleasant roasted aroma. Let cool and proceed with recipe.

Cookies

• BASLER BRUNSLI •

It's not that easy to find traditional Christmas cookies incorporating chocolate. Perhaps this is because so many traditional European Christmas cookies were developed long before chocolate made its appearance on the European continent. These are an exception. In Basel, Switzerland, great chocolate meringue cookies *are* a Christmas tradition.

8 ounces whole almonds
1 cup granulated sugar, plus
    additional sugar for rolling out
    meringue
4 ounces semisweet or bittersweet
    chocolate, finely grated
2 tablespoons Dutch process cocoa
    powder

½ teaspoon ground cinnamon
¼ teaspoon ground nutmeg
¼ teaspoon ground cloves
2 egg whites, at room temperature
⅛ teaspoon salt

1. Preheat oven to 450°F. Line 2 cookie sheets with parchment paper.

2. Place the almonds and 2 tablespoons of the sugar in the bowl of a food processor fitted with a steel blade. Process, pulsing on and off, until the almonds are finely ground.

3. In a medium-size bowl, whisk together the ground almonds, grated chocolate, cocoa, cinnamon, nutmeg, and cloves.

4. In the bowl of an electric mixer, beat the egg whites together with the salt, at medium speed, until soft peaks form. Raise speed to high and beat in the remaining sugar, 1 tablespoon at a time, until the egg whites are very

shiny and form stiff peaks. Use a large rubber spatula to fold the egg whites, in three additions, into the chocolate almond mixture.

5. Scrape the meringue onto a work surface sprinkled with about ¼ cup granulated sugar and spread it out to a thickness of ½ inch. Sprinkle the surface of the meringue with additional granulated sugar and roll it out with a rolling pin to an even thickness between ¼ and ½ inch. Cut the dough into small (approximately 1½-inch) squares or cut into small rounds with cookie cutters. Arrange on prepared cookie sheets and bake for 5 minutes.

6. Remove from oven and place cookie sheets on wire racks. Let cookies cool completely on the cookie sheets. Store the cookies in an airtight container at room temperature for up to 2 weeks, or freeze them for up to 2 months.

Yield: 2 dozen cookies

• CHOCOLATE LEBKUCHEN •

Spiced honey cakes are among the oldest and most popular Christmas treats in Germany and all over Europe. These Lebkuchen are brought up to date by giving them a dark chocolate glaze. The combination of honey, spices, and chocolate is divine and these make truly unusual and delicious gifts. Lebkuchen should be made at least 2 weeks in advance to allow the flavors to mellow, and they will keep for several months in an airtight container.

4 cups unbleached all-purpose
   flour
½ teaspoon baking soda
½ teaspoon baking powder
½ teaspoon salt
1 teaspoon ground cinnamon
½ teaspoon ground ginger
½ teaspoon ground cardamom
½ teaspoon crushed aniseed
¼ teaspoon ground nutmeg
¼ teaspoon ground cloves
1½ cups honey
½ cup firmly packed brown sugar

4 tablespoons unsalted butter
Grated zest of 1 orange
Grated zest of 1 lemon
¼ cup brandy, Cognac, or bourbon
2 large eggs, at room temperature
1½ cups whole toasted almonds,
   finely chopped
⅓ cup finely chopped golden raisins

For the Icing
4 ounces bittersweet or semisweet
   chocolate

1. In a large bowl, whisk together the flour, baking soda, baking powder, salt, cinnamon, ginger, cardamom, aniseed, nutmeg, and cloves.

2. In a medium-size saucepan, heat the honey, brown sugar, and butter over medium heat, stirring constantly, until the butter melts and the sugar

dissolves. Pour into the bowl of an electric mixer, stir in the orange zest, lemon zest, and the brandy, and let the mixture cool.

3. Using the paddle on your mixer, beat in the eggs, one at a time, until each is completely absorbed. Lower the speed and stir in the almonds and raisins. Stir in the flour mixture, ½ cup at a time.

4. Remove the dough to a lightly floured surface and knead it briefly until it is smooth and elastic. Divide the dough in half and pat each piece of dough into a rectangle about ½ inch thick. Wrap tightly in plastic wrap and refrigerate for at least 2 days, or for as long as 5 days. This allows the flavors to mellow and ripen.

5. Preheat oven to 350°F. Line 2 to 4 baking sheets with parchment paper.

6. Roll out each piece of dough on a lightly floured surface into a large (15 × 9-inch) rectangle ¼ inch thick. Cut the dough into 36 (1½ × 2½-inch) rectangles, cutting 6 strips each way. Arrange the cookies 1 inch apart on the prepared baking sheets.

7. Bake one sheet at a time for 15 to 20 minutes, or until lightly browned on top. Remove cookies to wire racks to cool completely.

8. Melt the chocolate in the top of a double boiler set over (but not touching) barely simmering water. Remove from the heat and set aside to cool slightly. Use a knife to spread a smooth covering of chocolate on one side of each Lebkuchen. Return to cooling racks, chocolate side up, until the chocolate has hardened completely.

9. Store the cookies in an airtight container at room temperature for at least 2 weeks and for as long as 2 months.

Yield: 6 dozen cookies

• PENNSYLVANIA DUTCH CHOCOLATE CHRISTMAS COOKIES •

Plain and simple and delicious. These are the kinds of cookies I like to have around all year. Pack them in a glass cookie jar and give them to someone you love.

1 cup whole wheat flour, * *sifted before measuring*
1½ cups unbleached all-purpose flour, sifted before measuring
1 cup Dutch process cocoa powder
1 teaspoon baking soda
1 teaspoon ground cinnamon

¼ teaspoon salt
2 sticks (½ pound) unsalted butter, softened to room temperature
2 cups granulated sugar
1 large egg, at room temperature
1 tablespoon brewed coffee
1 teaspoon vanilla extract

1. Preheat oven to 375°F. Line cookie sheets with parchment paper.
2. In a medium-size bowl, whisk together both flours, cocoa, baking soda, cinnamon, and salt.
3. In the bowl of an electric mixer, beat the butter and 1¾ cups of the sugar together until light and fluffy. Beat in the egg, coffee, and vanilla. On lowest speed, gradually mix in the dry ingredients to make a smooth dough.
4. Remove the dough to a lightly floured pastry cloth. Divide the dough

---

*I recommend King Arthur Flour white whole wheat flour, available in some supermarkets or by mail from The King Arthur Flour Baker's Catalogue (see sources, page 123).

in half. Roll out one half with a floured rolling pin, turning the dough over once, to a ¼-inch thickness. Cut out cookies with large (3-inch rounds are good) cookie cutters. Transfer to the cookie sheets with a large metal spatula. Arrange the cookies approximately 1 inch apart. Continue, lightly flouring the cloth as necessary, until all the dough has been made into cookies. Sprinkle the tops of the cookies with the remaining ¼ cup sugar.

5. Bake for 10 minutes. Cookies will still be soft when you remove them, but they will become crisp as they cool. Transfer the cookies to wire racks to cool completely. Store in an airtight container at room temperature for up to 2 weeks.

Yield: about 3 dozen cookies

The superiority of the article [chocolate] both for health and nourishment will soon give it the same preference over tea and coffee in America which it has in Spain.
                    —Thomas Jefferson, in a letter to John Adams,
                                        November 27, 1785

◆ REALLY GOOD CHOCOLATE CHIP COOKIES ◆

This is a handy recipe to have around for the holidays because it yields about 90 cookies in one baking session. When I need a gift for someone I don't know very well, or if I want to please a conservative child, these are the cookies I make. I've yet to meet someone who doesn't appreciate a good chocolate chip cookie.

3½ cups all-purpose flour
1½ teaspoons baking soda
1½ teaspoons salt
3 sticks (¾ pound) unsalted
* butter, softened to room*
* temperature*
1 cup granulated sugar, plus
* additional for topping*

1 cup firmly packed light brown sugar
3 large eggs, at room temperature
2 tablespoons vanilla extract
3 cups semisweet chocolate chips
1½ cups broken walnut pieces

1. Preheat oven to 350°F. Line several cookie sheets with parchment paper. You may need to use each cookie sheet more than once. Cool cookie sheet completely after each baking and reline with parchment paper.

2. In a large bowl, whisk together the flour, baking soda, and salt.

3. In the bowl of an electric mixer, beat the butter and both sugars until light and fluffy. Beat in eggs, one at a time, beating well after each addition. Beat in vanilla extract. Lower speed and gradually beat in the flour mixture until dough just comes together. Remove bowl from electric mixer and stir in chocolate chips and walnuts.

4. Drop the dough by tablespoonfuls about 2 inches apart on prepared cookie sheets. Wet the bottom of a glass tumbler, dip in granulated sugar, and press down on a cookie to flatten. Dip the glass in sugar to flatten each cookie.

5. Bake cookies for 10 to 12 minutes, until they are lightly browned. Remove cookies to wire racks and let cool completely. Store them in an airtight container at room temperature for up to 2 weeks.

Yield: about 90 cookies

How to Eat Like a Child

Chocolate-chip cookies: half-sit, half-lie on the bed, propped up by a pillow. Read a book. Place cookies next to you on the sheet so that crumbs get in the bed. As you eat the cookies, remove each chocolate chip and place it on your stomach. When all the cookies are consumed, eat the chips one by one, allowing two per page.

—Delia Ephron

• VERY CHOCOLATE CHOCOLATE CHIPPERS •

These are big, beautiful chocolate cookies loaded with chocolate chips and walnuts. What chocolate lover could resist? Pack a dozen gift cookies in a paper Chinese food container and save the remainder for yourself.

1 pound semisweet chocolate,
  coarsely chopped
4 tablespoons unsalted butter
1/2 cup cake flour
1 teaspoon baking powder
1 teaspoon instant espresso powder
1/4 teaspoon salt

4 large eggs, at room temperature
1 1/2 cups granulated sugar
1 tablespoon vanilla extract
2 cups (1 12-ounce package)
  semisweet chocolate chips
1 cup walnuts, toasted and coarsely
  chopped

1. Melt the chocolate and butter in the top of a double boiler set over (but not touching) barely simmering water. Remove from the heat and set aside to cool slightly.

2. In a small bowl, whisk together the cake flour, baking powder, espresso powder, and salt.

3. In the bowl of an electric mixer, beat the eggs and sugar together until pale and thick. Beat in the vanilla extract and melted chocolate. Reduce speed to low and stir in the flour mixture. Remove bowl from electric mixer and fold in the chocolate chips and the walnuts with a rubber spatula. Cover the bowl with plastic wrap and refrigerate for 30 minutes, until the batter is firm. (The batter can be refrigerated overnight.)

4. Preheat oven to 350°F. Line 2 cookie sheets with parchment paper.

5. Drop batter by ¼ cupfuls onto prepared cookie sheets. Press with moist fingertips to form 2½-to-3-inch rounds. Bake cookies for about 15 minutes, until the tops are dry and start to crack. Remove from oven and let cool on cookie sheets for 5 minutes. Transfer cookies to wire racks to cool completely. Store in airtight containers at room temperature for up to 2 weeks.

Yield: about 18 cookies

• COWBOY COOKIES •

In her wonderful book, *Maida Heatter's Book of Great Chocolate Desserts*, Ms. Heatter says, "In Colorado any oatmeal cookie that contains chocolate chips is called a Cowboy Cookie." In my experience cowboys and city slickers alike can enjoy these crisp, delicious cookies. Pack these in a cookie jar for a superb gift.

1½ cups unbleached all-purpose flour
1 teaspoon baking soda
½ teaspoon salt
2 sticks (½ pound) unsalted butter, softened to room temperature

1 cup firmly packed light brown sugar
½ cup granulated sugar
2 large eggs, at room temperature
2 teaspoons vanilla extract
2 cups rolled oats
2 cups semisweet chocolate chips
1 cup chopped walnuts

1. Preheat oven to 350°F. Line several cookie sheets with parchment paper. You may need to use each cookie sheet more than once. Cool cookie sheet completely after each baking and reline with parchment paper.

2. In a medium-size bowl, whisk together the flour, baking soda, and salt.

3. In the bowl of an electric mixer, beat together the butter and both sugars until very light and fluffy. Beat in the eggs, one at a time, until each is well blended. Beat in the vanilla extract. Reduce speed to low and gradually beat in the flour mixture. Remove bowl from electric mixer and stir in the rolled oats, chocolate chips, and walnuts. You will have a very stiff dough.

4. Drop heaping teaspoonfuls of dough onto the prepared cookie sheets, spacing the mounds 2 inches apart. Bake for 15 to 18 minutes, until cookies are golden. Transfer to wire cooling racks and let cool completely. Store cookies in an airtight container at room temperature for 3 to 4 weeks.

Yield: 4 to 5 dozen cookies

Chocolate is a French or Spanish article, and one seldom served on American tables.
> —Harriet Beecher Stowe, *The American Woman's Home or Principles of Domestic Sciences,* 1869

· INSIDE-OUT CHOCOLATE CHIP COOKIES ·

Several years ago I was taken to lunch at the Union Square Cafe, where I had a splendid meal and sampled a wonderfully inventive chocolate chip cookie: the cookie was chocolate and the chips were white chocolate. I went home and experimented with, I thought, great success. Later when a recipe for these cookies appeared in *The Union Square Cafe Cookbook*, I was pleased to see that I had come up with a pretty similar cookie. A great gift for anyone who loves chocolate chip cookies.

*1¾ cups unbleached all-purpose
  flour*
*1¼ cups Dutch process cocoa
  powder*
2 teaspoons baking soda
¼ teaspoon salt
*2½ sticks (½ pound plus 4
  tablespoons) unsalted butter,
  softened to room temperature*

1 cup granulated sugar
1 cup firmly packed dark brown sugar
2 large eggs, at room temperature
2 teaspoons vanilla extract
*10 ounces white chocolate, broken
  into ¼-inch chunks*

1. Preheat oven to 350°F. Line several cookie sheets with parchment paper. You may need to use each cookie sheet more than once. Cool cookie sheet completely after each baking and reline with parchment paper.

2. In a large bowl, whisk together the flour, cocoa powder, baking soda, and salt.

3. In the bowl of an electric mixer, beat the butter and sugars together

until light and fluffy. Beat in the eggs, one at a time, beating well after each addition. Beat in the vanilla. On low speed, beat in the flour mixture until completely incorporated. Remove bowl from the mixer and fold in the white chocolate chunks with a rubber spatula.

4. Drop tablespoonfuls of batter onto the prepared cookie sheets, leaving 2 inches between each cookie. Bake for 8 to 10 minutes, until cookies are puffed but still soft to the touch. Let cool for 5 minutes on baking sheets, then transfer cookies to wire racks to cool completely.

5. Store cookies in an airtight container at room temperature for up to 2 weeks.

Yield: about 5 dozen cookies

I bought my brother some gift-wrap for Christmas. I took it to the Gift Wrap department and told them to wrap it, but in a different print so he would know when to stop unwrapping.

—Steven Wright

◆ CHOCOLATE APRICOT CHIPPERS ◆

A scrumptious chocolate chip cookie that is made soft and chewy with the addition of rolled oats, shredded coconut, and Cognac-marinated apricot chunks. These are great to fill up a cookie jar, and make a welcome and satisfying gift. Try to marinate the apricots a day or two before you bake.

1 cup chopped dried apricots
½ cup Cognac or brandy
2 cups unbleached all-purpose
  flour
1 teaspoon baking soda
½ teaspoon salt
½ teaspoon ground cinnamon
½ teaspoon ground cloves
½ teaspoon ground nutmeg
2 sticks (½ pound) unsalted
  butter, softened to room
  temperature

1 cup firmly packed dark brown sugar
½ cup granulated sugar
2 large eggs, at room temperature
2 teaspoons vanilla extract
1 cup rolled oats
1 cup semisweet chocolate chips
½ cup unsweetened shredded coconut

1. One or two days before baking, place the chopped apricots and Cognac or brandy in a glass jar with a lid. Cover and let marinate until needed.

2. Preheat oven to 350°F. Line cookie sheets with parchment paper.

3. In a medium-size bowl, whisk together the flour, baking soda, salt, cinnamon, cloves, and nutmeg. Set aside.

4. In the bowl of an electric mixer, beat the butter and sugars together

until light and fluffy. Beat in the eggs, one at a time, and beat in the vanilla extract. Reduce speed to low and beat in the flour mixture until well combined. Remove bowl from mixer and stir in the drained apricots (brandy or Cognac is for you), rolled oats, chocolate chips, and shredded coconut. The dough will be very stiff.

5. Drop the dough by tablespoonfuls about 2 inches apart on prepared cookie sheets. Bake cookies for 10 to 12 minutes, until they are lightly browned. Remove cookies to wire racks and let cool completely. Store them in an airtight container at room temperature for up to 1 month.

Yield: 3 to 4 dozen cookies

· CHOCOLATE VANILLA SWIRL COOKIES ·

These lovely black and white cookies are great to have on hand, unbaked, tucked away in the freezer. When you need a last-minute Christmas gift, light the oven, slice the cookies, and bake them. Pop them into a colorful mylar bag, tie with a ribbon, and voilà!

1 ounce bittersweet chocolate
1½ cups unbleached all-purpose
   flour
1 teaspoon baking powder
¼ teaspoon salt
1 stick (¼ pound) unsalted butter,
   softened to room temperature

¾ cup granulated sugar
1 large egg plus 1 egg yolk, at room
   temperature
1 teaspoon vanilla extract

1. Melt the chocolate in the top of a double boiler set over (but not touching) barely simmering water. Remove from the heat and set aside to cool slightly.

2. In a small bowl, whisk together the flour, baking powder, and salt.

3. In the bowl of an electric mixer, cream the butter and sugar together at high speed until light and fluffy. Beat in the egg, egg yolk, and the vanilla extract. On low speed, gradually stir in the flour mixture until well combined.

4. Remove half of the dough and set aside on a sheet of waxed paper. Stir the melted chocolate into the remaining dough until well blended. Transfer the chocolate dough to the waxed paper and press the two doughs together to form a ball. Knead very briefly until the dough looks marbleized,

then shape the dough into a 12-inch log. Wrap tightly in plastic wrap and refrigerate for 2 to 3 hours, until very firm. (You may prefer to freeze the log to bake the cookies at a later date.)

5. Preheat oven to 375°F. Line 2 cookie sheets with parchment paper.

6. Cut the dough into ¼-inch slices and place them 1 inch apart on the prepared cookie sheets. Bake for 8 to 10 minutes, until the cookies are firm but not browned. Remove from oven and transfer the cookies to a wire rack to cool completely. Store the cookies in an airtight container at room temperature for up to 10 days.

Yield: about 3 dozen cookies

• BOURBON-LACED CHOCOLATE PECAN COOKIES •

A very grown-up cookie with a southern accent. Make these for a favorite uncle or any gentleman on your list.

1/2 cup raisins
1/2 cup bourbon
2 cups unbleached all-purpose flour
1/4 cup Dutch process cocoa powder
1 teaspoon baking soda
1/2 teaspoon baking powder
1/2 teaspoon salt

1 1/2 sticks (12 tablespoons) unsalted butter, softened to room temperature
1 cup firmly packed brown sugar
1 large egg, at room temperature
1/2 cup chopped pecans
48 pecan halves for decorating

1. Soak the raisins in the bourbon overnight. Drain the raisins and reserve raisins and bourbon.

2. Preheat oven to 350°F. Line 3 baking sheets with parchment paper.

3. In a medium-size bowl, whisk together the flour, cocoa, baking soda, baking powder, and salt.

4. In the bowl of an electric mixer, cream the butter and sugar until light and fluffy. Beat in the egg and reserved bourbon. Gradually stir in the flour mixture, followed by the raisins and pecans.

5. Drop dough by tablespoonfuls, 2 inches apart, onto the prepared cookie sheets. Press a pecan half into the center of each cookie.

6. Bake for 7 to 10 minutes, just until cookies feel springy to the touch

and have not yet browned around the edges. Remove from the oven and transfer cookies to wire racks to cool completely. Store cookies in airtight containers at room temperature for up to 2 weeks.

Yield: 4 dozen cookies

W hat's in a name?
Cacauatl, the Mexican name for cocoa; *xocoatl,* the Mexican name for chocolate; and *Theobromo cacao,* Linnaeus's botanical name for the cacao tree, all mean "food of the gods."

• CHOCOLATE TEDDY BEARS •

... o can resist a chocolate teddy bear? I like my bears very simple. Mini chocolate chips for eyes, nose, and buttons down the front. Press these into the cut-out cookies before baking. You may, of course, shape this simple cookie dough into pigs or cats or angels.

2½ cups all-purpose flour
2 teaspoons baking powder
½ cup Dutch process cocoa powder
1 teaspoon ground cinnamon
¼ teaspoon salt
1 stick (¼ pound) unsalted butter,
  softened to room temperature

1 cup granulated sugar
2 large eggs, at room temperature
1 teaspoon vanilla extract
Mini chocolate chips for decorating

1. In a medium-size bowl, whisk together the flour, baking powder, cocoa, cinnamon, and salt to blend. Set aside.

2. In the bowl of an electric mixer, beat butter and sugar together until light and fluffy. Beat in eggs, one at a time, and vanilla extract. On low speed, beat in flour mixture until just incorporated.

3. Divide dough in half and scoop out onto two sheets of plastic wrap. Using the plastic wrap, flatten the dough into large disks, wrap tightly, and refrigerate for 2 hours or overnight.

4. Preheat oven to 375°F. Line 2 or 3 baking sheets with parchment paper.

5. Remove the dough from refrigerator. Dust rolling pin with flour and

roll out dough on a lightly floured surface. Dough should be ¼-inch-to-⅛-inch thick. The thinner the dough the crisper the cookies. Cut out bears with cookie cutters dipped in flour. If you wish to use the cookies as hanging ornaments, make a hole in each cookie with the blunt end of a bamboo skewer or plastic straw. Press chocolate chips into the dough for eyes, buttons, etc. Transfer to prepared cookie sheets with a spatula.

6. Bake for 8 to 10 minutes, until cookies feel springy when touched. Remove from oven and transfer cookies to wire racks to cool. If the holes in the cookies have closed during baking, punch them out again with the blunt end of a bamboo skewer. Let cookies cool completely and store in an airtight container at room temperature for up to 1 month.

Yield: 1 to 3 dozen cookies, depending on size of cutters

◆ CHOCOLATE-FILLED ALMOND MERINGUES ◆

Don't be put off by the length of this recipe. It was a lot harder to write than these scrumptious meringues are to make. This is the gift to make for someone very special. Crunchy, nutty meringues surround a center of delicious chocolate ganache. They are truly impressive and irresistible. This is a gift to carry by hand. I would be loath to trust them to the mails.

Meringues
3/4 cup sliced almonds, toasted in
   a 325°F oven for 5 to 8
   minutes and cooled
2 tablespoons granulated sugar
3 large egg whites, at room
   temperature
1/4 teaspoon cream of tartar
1/4 cup superfine sugar

1/2 teaspoon almond extract
1/4 cup confectioners' sugar

Chocolate Filling
6 ounces semisweet or bittersweet
   chocolate, coarsely chopped
1/3 cup heavy cream
2 tablespoons butter

1. Line 2 baking sheets with parchment paper.

2. Place the sliced, toasted almonds and 2 tablespoons granulated sugar into the bowl of a food processor fitted with the metal blade. Pulse on and off until the almonds are ground to a fine meal.

3. In the bowl of an electric mixer fitted with a balloon whisk, beat the egg whites until frothy. Add the cream of tartar and beat at medium speed until soft peaks form. Gradually beat in the superfine sugar and beat until the egg whites are very stiff and glossy. Beat in the almond extract and remove bowl from electric mixer. Sift the confectioners' sugar over the egg

whites and use a wire whisk to fold in the confectioners' sugar and the ground almonds.

4. Scrape the meringue mixture into a reclosable quart-size plastic bag. Snip a ½-inch piece from one of the lower corners of the bag and pipe 1½-inch-high mounds of meringue onto the prepared baking sheets. You should get about 15 mounds per sheet. Let the mounds stand for 10 to 15 minutes, until they are slightly dry. Dip your index finger into confectioners' sugar and into the center of each meringue to make a depression about ½ inch wide. Let stand at room temperature for 1 hour to dry out.

5. Preheat oven to 200°F.

6. Bake for 1 hour, turn off the oven, and leave meringues in the oven for 1 hour longer. Remove from the oven and transfer to a wire rack to cool completely.

7. Melt the chocolate in the top of a double boiler set over (but not touching) barely simmering water. Stir the mixture occasionally with a rubber spatula. Remove top of double boiler from heat when most, but not all, of the chocolate is melted. Stir, until all the chocolate is melted and smooth. In a small saucepan, heat the heavy cream to the boiling point. Pour over the melted chocolate and stir until smooth. Stir in the butter until melted and smooth. Cover with plastic wrap and refrigerate until thickened, about 20 minutes.

8. Transfer the chocolate to a reclosable quart-size plastic bag. Snip off a small corner and pipe into the depressions in the meringues.

9. Store the chocolate-filled meringues in an airtight container at room temperature for up to 10 days.

Yield: about 30 meringues

· COCOA MERINGUE KISSES ·

These are cocoa-colored meringues with a surprise of chocolate chips. Because they can be made way ahead, they are a good item to have on hand for last-minute gifts. People who must adhere to a wheat-free diet will especially appreciate these.

4 large egg whites, at room temperature
1/2 teaspoon cream of tartar
1/2 cup superfine sugar

1/2 cup confectioners' sugar
3 tablespoons Dutch process cocoa powder
1 cup semisweet mini chocolate chips

1. Line 2 baking sheets with parchment paper.

2. In the bowl of an electric mixer fitted with a balloon whisk, beat the egg whites until frothy. Add the cream of tartar and beat at medium speed until soft peaks form. Gradually beat in the superfine sugar and beat until the egg whites are very stiff and glossy. Remove bowl from electric mixer. Sift the confectioners' sugar and cocoa over the egg whites, and use a wire whisk to fold them into the egg whites. Finally, fold in the chocolate chips.

3. Using a tablespoon, scoop up mounds about 2 inches high and place them on the prepared baking sheets at least 1 inch apart. Let dry for 30 minutes at room temperature.

4. Preheat oven to 200°F.

5. Bake for 2 hours. The meringues should not begin to color. Turn off the oven and leave them inside for an hour longer. Remove and transfer

the meringues to wire racks to cool completely. Store in airtight containers at room temperature for up to 2 months.

Yield: about 2 dozen meringue kisses

A QUICK HISTORY OF CHOCOLATE

Chocolate was for many centuries enjoyed chiefly as a beverage. Its popularity began in the Americas, where the cacao tree grew wild. In the early 1500s when Hernando Cortez conquered Mexico, the Aztec emperor Montezuma served him a drink called chocolatl. Cortez brought the beverage back to Spain. With sugar, vanilla, and cinnamon added to sweeten the bitter drink, it became a favorite with the Spanish aristocracy. In the 1600s the drink won popularity among the upper classes in France and England. In 1753 the botanist Carolus Linnaeus gave the cacao tree the botanical name *Theobroma,* meaning "food of the gods." In the 1800s the processes for making smooth, tasty eating chocolate were invented. This increased the popularity of chocolate products further. Today the chocolate industry in the United States is a big one, absorbing more than one fourth of the world production of cacao beans. Other important manufacturing countries are Germany, The Netherlands, Great Britain, and France.

—from *Compton's Encyclopedia*

• CHOCOLATE ALMOND COCOA CRESCENTS •

Everyone loves these light and crumbly cookies. You can leave them alone after you've dusted them with confectioners' sugar or you can make them very special by covering half of each cookie with chocolate. Although they are fragile, I have shipped them successfully by layering them very carefully in lots of crumpled tissue paper.

1½ cups cake flour
2 tablespoons Dutch process cocoa
    powder
Pinch of salt
¾ cup confectioners' sugar
¾ cup blanched slivered almonds,
    toasted in the oven at 325°F for
    5 to 10 minutes

½ cup granulated sugar
2 sticks (½ pound) unsalted butter
1 egg yolk
1 teaspoon vanilla extract
6 ounces semisweet or bittersweet
    chocolate (optional)

1. In a small bowl, whisk together the flour, cocoa powder, and salt and set aside. Put the confectioners' sugar in a wide shallow bowl and set aside.

2. In the bowl of a food processor fitted with a metal blade, combine the almonds and 2 tablespoons of the granulated sugar. Pulse on and off until the nuts are ground to a fine meal.

3. Beat the butter with a rolling pin to soften. In the bowl of an electric mixer, beat the butter and remaining granulated sugar together until very light and fluffy. Beat in the yolk and vanilla extract. Reduce speed to low and beat in the ground nuts, followed by the flour mixture. Scrape the

dough out of the bowl and onto a sheet of plastic wrap. Shape into a disk, wrap tightly, and refrigerate for 30 minutes to 1 hour.

4. Preheat oven to 350°F. Line 2 baking sheets with parchment paper.

5. Remove the dough from the refrigerator to a lightly floured surface. Divide the dough into 10 pieces. Roll each piece into a slender rope, about ½ inch in diameter. Cut each rope into approximately 2½-inch lengths. Shape into crescents and arrange them on the prepared baking sheets. Bake for 15 to 20 minutes, until the cookies are firm and just beginning to color. Remove from the oven and let the cookies cool on the baking sheets for several minutes. Using a metal spatula, transfer the cookies, a few at a time, to the confectioners' sugar and roll them gently in the sugar to cover. Place powdered cookies on wire racks to cool completely.

6. The next step is optional, but if you would like to dip the cookies in chocolate, proceed as follows: Melt the chocolate in the top of a double boiler set over (but not touching) barely simmering water. Stir the mixture occasionally with a rubber spatula. Remove top of double boiler from heat when most, but not all, of the chocolate is melted. Stir until all the chocolate is melted and smooth. Dip each cookie halfway into the chocolate and place on foil or waxed paper. Continue until all are done. Let stand until chocolate hardens and surface dulls.

7. Store the cookies in an airtight container at room temperature for up to 1 month.

Yield: 3 to 4 dozen cookies

I generally avoid temptation unless I can't resist it.
—Mae West, in *My Little Chickadee*

• CHOCOLATE ALMOND MACAROONS •

These cookies may not be great keepers, but they are so quick and easy to make that you can almost make up batches as you need them. A perfect gift for someone with wheat allergies, or anyone at all who loves the combination of almond and chocolate.

2 cups blanched slivered almonds, toasted in the oven at 325°F for 5 to 10 minutes
1 cup granulated sugar
¼ teaspoon ground cinnamon
Pinch of salt

1 large egg, at room temperature
2 large egg whites, at room temperature
¼ teaspoon almond extract
3 ounces semisweet or bittersweet chocolate, very finely chopped or grated

1. Preheat oven to 350°F. Line 2 baking sheets with parchment paper.
2. In the bowl of a food processor fitted with a metal blade, combine the almonds, sugar, cinnamon, and salt. Process until finely ground. Add egg, egg whites, and almond extract and process until mixture holds together. Scrape into a medium-size bowl and stir in the chocolate.
3. Moisten your hands and roll mixture into walnut-size balls. Place on prepared baking sheets. Use the bottom of a glass tumbler to flatten each ball to a round approximately ⅓ inch thick. Bake for 12 to 15 minutes, until tops are puffy but the centers are still soft. Transfer cookies to a wire rack and let cool completely. Store in an airtight container at room temperature for up to 5 days.

Yield: about 2 dozen macaroons

An Abundance of Brownies

· GRAND MARNIER BROWNIES ·

The combination of chocolate and orange is a classic one for the sophisticated palate, making these very grown-up and sophisticated brownies indeed. They make a wonderful finish for an elegant dinner, and I particularly like to serve them with a bowl of peeled and sectioned clementines. And here's a great gift idea: pack up individually wrapped brownies in a tin or box and present them as a gift, along with a crate of the wonderful clementines, which are so conveniently in season during the holidays.

15 ounces bittersweet chocolate,
   coarsely chopped
1½ sticks (12 tablespoons)
   unsalted butter
½ cup granulated sugar
3 large eggs, at room temperature
⅓ cup Grand Marnier

1 teaspoon vanilla extract
1 teaspoon finely grated orange zest
½ teaspoon orange oil★ (optional)
1¼ cups all-purpose flour
¼ teaspoon salt
1½ cups broken-up walnut halves

1. Preheat oven to 350°F. Lightly grease the bottom and sides of a 13 × 9 × 2-inch baking pan and line the bottom with parchment paper.

★Boyajian, Inc., of Newton, Massachusetts, is the purveyor of excellent citrus oils—orange, lemon, and lime. They are superb products, completely natural, each essence squeezed from the rind of the fresh fruit. They are available by mail from The King Arthur Flour Baker's Catalogue or from Williams-Sonoma (see sources, page 123).

2. Melt the chocolate and butter in the top of a double boiler set over (but not touching) barely simmering water. Stir the mixture occasionally with a rubber spatula. Remove top of double boiler from heat when most, but not all, of the chocolate is melted. Stir until all the chocolate is melted and smooth. Set aside to cool.

3. In the bowl of an electric mixer, beat the sugar and eggs together, at high speed, until pale and thick. Beat in 4 tablespoons of the Grand Marnier, the vanilla extract, orange zest, and orange oil until just combined. Beat in the melted chocolate. On low speed, stir in the flour and salt just until mixed. Stir in the broken nuts.

4. Scrape the batter into the prepared pan and bake for 25 to 30 minutes, until the top feels firm when touched lightly, but a cake tester inserted into the center comes out coated with fudgy crumbs. Do not overbake.

5. Remove the brownies from the oven and place the pan on a wire rack to cool. While they are still hot, brush the surface with the remaining Grand Marnier. Cover the pan tightly with foil and let cool completely. Cut the brownies into 30 squares and wrap each square in plastic wrap. Store them in an airtight container at room temperature for up to 1 week, or freeze them for up to 2 months.

Yield: 30 brownies

• RAIN FOREST BROWNIES •

I love the rich, suave flavor of Brazil nuts, and it's a good feeling to know that purchasing these nuts helps support a renewable resource of the Amazonian rain forest. These brownies are bursting with so many great flavors from the tropics that they are a good reminder of the hot sun, which seems to be in hiding at this time of year.

8 ounces bittersweet chocolate,
  coarsely chopped
2 sticks (½ pound) unsalted butter
½ cup unbleached all-purpose
  flour
½ cup cake flour
2 tablespoons cornstarch
½ teaspoon baking powder

½ teaspoon salt
1 cup granulated sugar
4 large eggs, at room temperature
1 teaspoon vanilla extract
2 tablespoons dark rum
1 cup chopped Brazil nuts
1 cup shredded sweetened coconut
1 cup raisins

1. Preheat oven to 350°F. Line a 13 × 9 × 2-inch pan with a double thickness of aluminum foil so that the foil extends 2 inches beyond the two short ends of the pan. Lightly butter the bottom and sides of the foil-lined pan.

2. Melt the chocolate and butter in the top of a double boiler set over (but not touching) barely simmering water. Stir the mixture occasionally with a rubber spatula. Remove top of double boiler from heat when most, but not all, of the chocolate is melted. Stir until all the chocolate is melted and smooth. Set aside to cool.

3. In a medium-size bowl, whisk together both of the flours, the cornstarch, baking powder, and salt. Set aside.

4. In the bowl of an electric mixer, beat the sugar and eggs together, at high speed, until thick and pale. Beat in the vanilla extract and rum. On low speed, beat in the melted chocolate until just combined. Stir in the flour mixture until mixed. Remove bowl from the mixer and stir in the Brazil nuts, shredded coconut, and raisins.

5. Scrape the batter into the prepared pan and bake the brownies for 30 to 35 minutes, until the top feels firm when touched lightly, but a cake tester inserted into the center comes out coated with fudgy crumbs. Do not overbake.

6. Remove from the oven and let cool completely. Lift the cake out of the pan and wrap completely in more aluminum foil. Refrigerate for several hours or overnight.

7. Remove from the refrigerator, unwrap, and invert the brownies onto a cutting board or large plate. Carefully peel off the foil. Invert again onto a smooth surface and cut with a serrated knife into large or small bars to make 24 or 32 brownies. Wrap them individually in plastic wrap and store in an airtight container at room temperature for a week to 10 days, or freeze them for up to 2 months.

Yield: 24 or 32 brownies

• ROASTED ALMOND BROWNIES •

Anyone who loves the combination of chocolate and almonds will adore these very fudgy, almost candylike brownies. The large amount of chocolate and whole roasted almonds impart a very luxurious quality, and the almond slices are very beautiful embedded in the chocolate bars.

4 ounces unsweetened chocolate,
    coarsely chopped
4 ounces bittersweet or semisweet
    chocolate, coarsely chopped
2 sticks (½ pound) unsalted butter
2 cups granulated sugar
5 large eggs, at room temperature

1 tablespoon vanilla extract
1 teaspoon almond extract
1⅔ cups unbleached all-purpose
    flour, sifted before measuring
¼ teaspoon salt
2 cups whole almonds, toasted in the
    oven at 325°F for 15 minutes

1. Preheat the oven to 350°F. Line a 13 × 9 × 2-inch pan with a double thickness of aluminum foil so that the foil extends 2 inches beyond the two short ends of the pan. Lightly butter the bottom and sides of the foil-lined pan.

2. Melt the two chocolates and butter in the top of a double boiler set over (but not touching) barely simmering water. Stir the mixture occasionally with a rubber spatula. Remove top of double boiler from heat when most, but not all, of the chocolate is melted. Stir until all the chocolate is melted and smooth. Set aside to cool.

3. In the bowl of an electric mixer, beat the sugar and eggs together, at high speed, until thick and pale. Beat in the vanilla and almond extracts.

On low speed, beat in the melted chocolate until just combined. Stir in the flour and salt just until mixed. Stir in the almonds with a wooden spoon.

4. Scrape the batter into the prepared pan and bake for 30 to 35 minutes, until the top feels firm when touched lightly, but a cake tester inserted into the center comes out coated with fudgy crumbs. Do not overbake.

5. Remove from the oven and place pan on a wire rack to cool completely. Lift the cake out of the pan and wrap tightly in more aluminum foil. Refrigerate for several hours or overnight.

6. Remove from the refrigerator, unwrap, and invert the brownies onto a cutting board or large plate. Carefully peel off the foil. Invert again onto a smooth surface and cut with a serrated knife into large or small bars to make 24 or 32 brownies. Wrap them individually in plastic wrap and store in an airtight container at room temperature for a week to 10 days, or freeze them for up to 2 months.

Yield: 24 or 32 brownies

As with most fine things, chocolate has its season. There is a simple memory aid that you can use to determine whether it is the correct time to order chocolate dishes: Any month whose name contains the letter a, e or u is the proper time for chocolate.

—Sandra Boynton, *Chocolate: The Consuming Passion*

• TRIPLE CHOCOLATE HAZELNUT BROWNIES •

6 ounces bittersweet or semisweet
  chocolate, coarsely chopped
4 ounces unsweetened chocolate,
  coarsely chopped
10 tablespoons unsalted butter, cut
  into 1-inch pieces
$^1\!/_2$ cup cake flour
1 teaspoon baking powder

$^1\!/_4$ teaspoon salt
5 large eggs, at room temperature
$1^1\!/_2$ cups granulated sugar
1 tablespoon vanilla extract
12 ounces white chocolate, cut into
  small chunks
2 cups toasted hazelnuts, coarsely
  chopped

1. Preheat oven to 350°F. Line a $13 \times 9 \times 2$-inch pan with a double thickness of aluminum foil so that the foil extends 2 inches beyond the two short ends of the pan. Lightly butter the bottom and sides of the foil-lined pan.

2. Melt the two chocolates and the butter in the top of a double boiler set over (but not touching) barely simmering water. Stir the mixture occasionally with a rubber spatula. Remove top of double boiler from heat when most, but not all, of the chocolate is melted. Stir until all the chocolate is melted and smooth. Set aside to cool.

3. In a small bowl, whisk together the flour, baking powder, and salt. Set aside.

4. In the bowl of an electric mixer, beat the eggs and sugar together, at high speed, until thick and pale. Beat in the vanilla extract. On low speed, beat in the melted chocolate until just combined. Stir in the flour mixture until mixed. Remove bowl from the mixer and fold in the white chocolate pieces and hazelnuts.

5. Scrape the batter into the prepared pan and bake for 20 to 25 minutes, until the top feels firm when touched lightly, but a cake tester inserted into the center comes out coated with fudgy crumbs. Do not overbake.

6. Cool the brownies in the pan set on a wire rack for 30 minutes. Using the two ends of the foil as handles, lift the brownies out of the pan. Cool the brownies on the foil for at least 2 hours.

7. Invert the brownies onto a cutting board or large plate and gently peel off the foil. Invert again onto a smooth surface and cut into 24 or 32 brownies. Wrap them individually in plastic wrap and store in an airtight container at room temperature for a week to 10 days, or freeze them for up to 2 months.

Yield: 24 or 32 brownies

Mail your packages early so the post office can lose them in time for Christmas.

—Johnny Carson

• HONEY BROWNIES •

The honey in these brownies adds a subtle and mysterious flavor and improves their keeping quality as well. These are terrific Christmas gifts to send to faraway chocolate lovers.

3 ounces unsweetened chocolate
6 tablespoons unsalted butter
1/2 cup honey
3/4 cup cake flour
1/2 teaspoon baking powder

1/4 teaspoon salt
1/2 cup granulated sugar
3 large eggs, at room temperature
1 teaspoon vanilla extract
3/4 cup chopped walnuts

1. Preheat oven to 325°F. Lightly grease the bottom and sides of a 13 × 9 × 2-inch pan and line the bottom with parchment paper.

2. Place the chocolate, butter, and honey in the top of a double boiler set over (but not touching) barely simmering water. Stir the mixture occasionally with a rubber spatula. Remove top of double boiler from heat when most, but not all, of the chocolate is melted. Stir until all the chocolate is melted and smooth. Set aside to cool.

3. In a medium-size bowl, whisk together the flour, baking powder, and salt.

4. In the bowl of an electric mixer, beat the sugar and eggs together, at high speed, until thick and pale. Beat in the vanilla extract. Remove bowl from electric mixer and alternately fold in the melted chocolate and flour until just combined. Fold in the walnuts.

5. Scrape the batter into the prepared pan and bake for 30 to 35 minutes,

until the top feels firm when touched lightly, but a cake tester inserted into the center comes out coated with fudgy crumbs. Do not overbake.

6. Remove pan from the oven and place on a wire rack to cool completely. Run a sharp knife around the edges of the pan and invert the brownies onto a cutting board or large plate. Peel away the parchment paper. Invert again onto a smooth surface and cut into 16 squares or 32 rectangles. Wrap each brownie tightly in plastic wrap and store in an airtight container at room temperature for up to 1 week, or up to 2 months in the freezer.

Yield: 16 or 32 brownies

My first encounter with chocolate came when I was a toddler, teething deliriously on my mother's brittle and intense squares of fudge.
—Marcel Desaulniers, *Death by Chocolate*

• CHOCOLATE CHUNK BLONDIES •

These are rich butterscotch brownies bursting with dark chocolate chunks. My husband, who sees no reason to "mess around with regular chocolate brownies," overcame his conservatism and found them "really good."

1 cup all-purpose flour
1½ cups cake flour
2 teaspoons baking powder
½ teaspoon salt
1½ sticks (12 tablespoons)
unsalted butter, softened to room
temperature

2 cups firmly packed brown sugar
⅓ cup granulated sugar
3 large eggs, at room temperature
2 teaspoons vanilla extract
12 ounces semisweet or bittersweet
chocolate, cut into chunks
1 cup chopped walnuts

1. Preheat oven to 350°F. Butter the bottom and sides of a 13 × 9 × 2-inch pan and line the bottom with parchment paper.

2. In a medium-size bowl, whisk together both flours, the baking powder, and salt. Set aside.

3. In the bowl of an electric mixer, beat the butter and both sugars at high speed until light and fluffy. Beat in the eggs, one at a time, until well combined. Beat in the vanilla extract. Change speed to low and gradually beat in the the flour until just combined. Remove bowl from the electric mixer and fold in the chocolate chunks and walnuts.

4. Scrape the batter into the prepared pan and bake for 40 to 45 minutes, until the top feels firm when touched lightly and a cake tester inserted into the center comes out clean.

5. Remove pan from the oven and place on a wire rack to cool completely. Run a sharp knife around the edges of the pan and invert the blondies onto a cutting board or large plate. Peel away the parchment paper. Invert again onto a smooth surface and cut into 24 or 32 bars. Wrap each blondie tightly in plastic wrap and store in an airtight container at room temperature for up to 1 week, or up to 2 months in the freezer.

Yield: 24 or 32 blondies

I love chocolate. I love the way it comes wrapped in thin silvery foil and heavy-grade paper, and the way it is molded into little squares and signed with the manufacturer's name. I love the way it smells and the way it feels in my mouth. I love the fact that the same piece of chocolate has different tastes depending on where in your mouth you eat it. I love the fulfilling and important feeling you get when you eat it. I love the idea of chocolate. It is a special food that fits into no category or niche. It is in a category by itself.

—Lora Brody, *Growing Up on the Chocolate Diet*

Brazil nuts come from large trees that grow along the Amazon River in Brazil. Their shells are very hard and therefore difficult to remove. I buy my Brazil nuts by mail from Walnut Acres Organic Farms. Their nuts are "hand-gathered and hand-shelled." They are raised without chemicals and are an excellent source of phosphorous and unsaturated oils. Store them, like other nuts, tightly wrapped in the freezer and toast them for 15 minutes in a 350°F oven to bring out their best flavor.

Bundles of Biscotti

• CHOCOLATE CHERRY BISCOTTI •

Is there a more heavenly combination than chocolate with cherries? I don't think so. Here the intense flavors of dried cherries and kirsch transform what might be a dull, dry cookie into a delicious indulgence. When you consider that they are very low in fat, these biscotti might become a permanent addition to your cookie jar. For an extravagant Christmas gift, buy a clear glass biscotti jar (I found mine at Williams-Sonoma) and load it up with Chocolate Cherry Biscotti.

2 tablespoons kirsch	*1 teaspoon baking powder*
1 cup dried cherries	*½ teaspoon salt*
1½ cups unbleached all-purpose	*2 large eggs, at room temperature*
* flour*	*1 cup granulated sugar*
½ cup Dutch process cocoa powder	*1 teaspoon vanilla extract*

1. Preheat oven to 350°F. Line a cookie sheet with parchment paper and set aside. Sprinkle the kirsch over the cherries and set aside.

2. In a medium bowl, whisk together the flour, cocoa, baking powder, and salt.

3. In the bowl of an electric mixer, beat the eggs, sugar, and vanilla for 3 minutes, until the mixture is very pale and thick. Stir in the flour mixture and the cherries to make a stiff dough.

4. Divide the dough in half. Wet your hands. On the prepared cookie sheet, shape each half into a log 12 to 14 inches long and 2 inches wide. Leave a space of at least 4 inches between the logs.

5. Bake for 30 minutes, until the logs are firm to the touch and beginning to crack on top.

6. Remove from oven (leave the oven on) and place the cookie sheet on a wire rack. Loosen logs with a metal spatula and let cool for 10 minutes.

7. Slide baked logs onto a cutting board. With a long serrated knife, cut each log diagonally, with a gentle sawing motion, into ½-inch slices. Arrange the biscotti, cut-side down, on the cookie sheet. Bake for 15 minutes, turning the biscotti over once, until they are dry and crisp. Remove the biscotti to a wire rack and let cool completely. Store them in an airtight container at room temperature for up to 1 month.

Yield: 3 to 4 dozen biscotti

• CHOCOLATE BRAZIL NUT BISCOTTI •

I love making these biscotti with whole Brazil nuts. Once the biscotti are sliced they are very dramatic looking—the large white ovals punctuating the very dark chocolate. You may substitute whole, unblanched roasted almonds if you wish for an equally delicious biscotto.

4 ounces bittersweet or semisweet chocolate, coarsely chopped
2 cups unbleached all-purpose flour
½ cup Dutch process cocoa powder
1½ teaspoons baking powder
½ teaspoon salt

¼ teaspoon ground cinnamon
1 cup granulated sugar
3 large eggs, at room temperature
1 teaspoon vanilla extract
2 teaspoons dark rum
1 cup whole Brazil nuts, toasted in a 325°F oven for 15 minutes

1. Preheat oven to 350° F. Line a baking sheet with parchment paper.

2. Melt the chocolate in the top of a double boiler set over (but not touching) barely simmering water. Remove from the heat, stir until smooth, and set aside to cool slightly.

3. In a medium-size bowl, whisk together the flour, cocoa, baking powder, salt, and cinnamon.

4. In the bowl of an electric mixer, beat the sugar and eggs together at high speed until pale and thick. Beat in the vanilla extract and dark rum. Reduce speed to low and gradually stir in the melted chocolate. Gradually stir in the flour mixture. Stir in the nuts with a wooden spoon and divide the dough in half. It will be rather sticky.

5. Place each dough half on a large piece of plastic wrap. Bring up the sides of the plastic and shape the dough into logs 12 to 14 inches long. Unroll the logs onto the prepared baking sheet, using a spatula to scrape the dough away from the plastic. Leave 3 to 4 inches between each log. With your hand wrapped in plastic, pat the tops smooth and flatten slightly. Bake for 30 minutes, until the logs are firm to the touch and the tops are beginning to show cracks.

6. Remove from oven (leave the oven on but reduce heat to 325°F) and place the cookie sheet on wire racks. Loosen logs with a metal spatula and let cool for 10 minutes.

7. Slide baked logs onto a cutting board. With a long serrated knife, cut each log diagonally, with a gentle sawing motion, into 1/2-inch slices. Arrange the biscotti, cut-side down, on the cookie sheets. Bake for 7 to 8 minutes, turn the cookies over, and bake for another 7 to 8 minutes. Remove the biscotti to a wire rack and let cool completely. Store them in an airtight container at room temperature for up to 1 month.

Yield: about 3 dozen biscotti

⋆ CHOCOLATE CHIP BISCOTTI ⋆

These biscotti will remind you of chocolate chip cookies, but with a lot less fat. Although in my experience children are not usually crazy about biscotti (too dry and plain), they usually make an exception for these. Especially if encouraged to dunk the biscotti in a glass of milk. I would definitely include these in any selection of cookies to give for Christmas. Or wrap them up, a dozen at a time, in shiny mylar and hand them out to your delivery people, child's teacher, your butcher, or your co-workers.

2 cups unbleached all-purpose
  flour
½ teaspoon baking soda
¼ teaspoon salt
2 large eggs, at room temperature
½ cup granulated sugar

½ cup firmly packed dark brown
  sugar
1 teaspoon vanilla extract
1 cup semisweet chocolate chips
½ cup chopped pecans

1. Preheat oven to 350°F. Line 2 cookie sheets with parchment paper.

2. In a medium-size bowl, whisk together the flour, baking soda, and salt.

3. In the bowl of an electric mixer, beat the eggs and sugars together at high speed until pale and thick. Beat in the vanilla extract, reduce speed to low, and stir in the flour mixture until just combined. Remove bowl from mixer and stir in the chocolate chips and pecans.

4. Divide the dough into thirds and arrange in 12-inch logs directly on the prepared cookie sheets. Leave at least 3 inches between the logs. Pat

the tops smooth and flatten slightly. Bake for 30 minutes, until the logs are firm to the touch and the tops are beginning to show cracks.

5. Remove from oven (leave the oven on but reduce heat to 325°F) and place the cookie sheets on wire racks. Loosen logs with a metal spatula and let cool for 10 minutes.

6. Slide baked logs onto a cutting board. With a long serrated knife, cut each log diagonally, with a gentle sawing motion, into ½-inch slices. Arrange the biscotti, cut-side down, on the cookie sheets. Bake for 7 to 8 minutes, turn the biscotti over, and bake for another 7 to 8 minutes, until they are dry and crisp. Remove the biscotti to a wire rack and let cool completely. Store the biscotti in an airtight container at room temperature for up to 1 month.

Yield: 4 dozen biscotti

I don't have to watch my figure as I never had much of one to watch. What you see before you is the result of a lifetime of chocolate.
— Katharine Hepburn, quoted in *Time* magazine,
November 17, 1980

• CHOCOLATE CHIP ORANGE-WALNUT BISCOTTI •

As if the heavenly combination of walnuts and chocolate chips wasn't enough, these luscious biscotti are permeated with the flavor and scent of orange. These biscotti are also more tender and richer in flavor because of their butter content. They make elegant Christmas presents on their own or in combination with other biscotti or cookies.

2 cups all-purpose flour
½ cup Dutch process cocoa powder
1 teaspoon grated orange zest
1 teaspoon baking soda
1 teaspoon salt
6 tablespoons unsalted butter, softened to room temperature

1 cup granulated sugar
2 large eggs, at room temperature
2 tablespoons Grand Marnier
¾ cup semisweet chocolate chips
1 cup walnuts, chopped
2 tablespoons confectioners' sugar

1. Preheat oven to 350°F. Line a cookie sheet with parchment paper.

2. In a medium-size bowl, whisk together the flour, cocoa, orange zest, baking soda, and salt.

3. In the bowl of an electric mixer, beat the butter and sugar until light and fluffy. Beat in the eggs, one at a time, until well combined. Beat in the Grand Marnier. Reduce speed to low and stir in the flour mixture to make a smooth dough. Remove bowl from the mixer and stir in the chocolate chips and walnuts.

4. Divide the dough in half. On the prepared cookie sheet, shape the

dough into logs, 12 to 14 inches long and 2 inches wide, leaving 3 to 4 inches between them. Sprinkle the tops with the confectioners' sugar. Pat the tops smooth and flatten slightly. Bake for 30 minutes, until the logs are firm to the touch and the tops are beginning to show cracks.

5. Remove from oven (leave the oven on but reduce heat to 325°F) and place the cookie sheet on a wire rack. Loosen logs with a metal spatula and let cool for 10 minutes.

6. Slide baked logs onto a cutting board. With a long serrated knife, cut each log diagonally, with a gentle sawing motion, into ½-inch slices. Arrange the biscotti, cut-side down, on the cookie sheet. Bake for 7 to 8 minutes, turn the biscotti, and bake for another 7 to 8 minutes, until they are dry and crisp. Remove the biscotti to a wire rack and let cool completely.

7. Store the biscotti in an airtight container at room temperature for up to 1 month.

Yield: about 30 biscotti

• SPICY CHOCOLATE PEAR BISCOTTI •

I love encountering a little bit of chewy dried fruit in an otherwise dry and hard biscotto. Here the combination of cocoa, spices, and dried pears is a happy one and particularly suited for the Christmas season.

2 cups unbleached all-purpose
   flour
1/4 cup Dutch process cocoa powder
1 teaspoon baking powder
1/2 teaspoon baking soda
1/2 teaspoon ground cinnamon
1/2 teaspoon ground allspice

1/4 teaspoon salt
1/4 teaspoon ground white pepper
1/4 teaspoon ground ginger
1 cup granulated sugar
3 large eggs, at room temperature
1 teaspoon vanilla extract
1 cup finely chopped dried pears

1. Preheat oven to 350°F. Line a cookie sheet with parchment paper.

2. In a medium-size bowl, whisk together the flour, cocoa, baking powder, baking soda, cinnamon, allspice, salt, pepper, and ginger.

3. In the bowl of an electric mixer, beat the sugar and eggs together until the mixture is very pale and thick. Beat in the vanilla extract.

4. Sift the dry ingredients over the egg mixture and fold in until the dough is just combined. Fold in the dried pears. Divide the dough in half. On the prepared cookie sheet, shape each half into a log 12 to 14 inches long and 2 inches wide. Leave a space of at least 4 inches between the logs.

5. Bake for about 30 minutes, until the loaves are firm to the touch and just beginning to crack on top.

6. Remove from oven (leave the oven on) and place the cookie sheet on a wire rack. Loosen logs with a metal spatula and let cool for 10 minutes.

7. Slide baked logs onto a cutting board. With a long serrated knife, cut each log diagonally, with a gentle sawing motion, into ½-inch slices. Arrange the biscotti, cut-side down, on the cookie sheet. Bake for 7 to 8 minutes, turn the biscotti over once, and bake for another 7 to 8 minutes, until they are dry and crisp. Remove the biscotti to a wire rack and let cool completely. Store them in an airtight container at room temperature for up to 1 month.

Yield: about 4 dozen biscotti

Chocolate can be lethal to dogs. Theobromine, an ingredient that stimulates the cardiac muscle and the central nervous system, causes chocolate's toxicity. About two ounces of milk chocolate can be poisonous for a ten-pound puppy.

• DOUBLE CHOCOLATE ALMOND BISCOTTI •

This recipe started its life in *Maida Heatter's Best Dessert Book Ever* and evolved over time. Any recipe from Maida Heatter is a great recipe and this one is no exception. Make up several batches to have on hand for the holidays and to give away as impromptu gifts.

2 cups unbleached all-purpose
flour, sifted before measuring
1/3 cup Dutch process cocoa powder
2 tablespoons instant espresso or
coffee powder
1 1/2 teaspoons baking powder
1/4 teaspoon salt
4 ounces semisweet or bittersweet
chocolate, coarsely chopped

3 large eggs, at room temperature
1 cup granulated sugar
1 teaspoon vanilla extract
1/2 teaspoon almond extract
1 1/2 cups whole unblanched almonds,
toasted

1. Preheat oven to 350°F. Line a cookie sheet with parchment paper.

2. In a medium-size bowl, whisk together the flour, cocoa, espresso or coffee powder, baking powder, and salt.

3. Place the chocolate together with 1/2 cup of the flour mixture in the bowl of a food processor fitted with the metal blade. Process for a minute or so until the chocolate is very finely grated. Remove from processor and whisk together with the flour mixture.

4. In the bowl of an electric mixer, beat the eggs and sugar together until pale and thick. Beat in the vanilla and almond extracts. Reduce speed and gradually stir in the flour-chocolate mixture. Stir in the almonds.

5. Divide the dough in half. On the prepared cookie sheet, shape each half into a log 12 to 14 inches long and 2 inches wide. Leave a space of at least 4 inches between the logs.

6. Bake for 30 minutes, until the loaves are firm to the touch and beginning to crack on top.

7. Remove from oven (leave the oven on) and place the cookie sheet on a wire rack. Loosen logs with a metal spatula and let cool for 10 minutes.

8. Slide baked logs onto a cutting board. With a long serrated knife, cut each log diagonally, with a gentle sawing motion, into ½-to-¾-inch slices. Arrange the biscotti, cut-side down, on the cookie sheet. Bake for 7 to 8 minutes, turn the biscotti over once, and bake for another 7 to 8 minutes, until they are dry and crisp. Remove the biscotti to a wire rack and let cool completely. Store them in an airtight container at room temperature for about 1 month.

Yield: about 4 dozen biscotti

If any man has drunk a little too deeply from the cup of physical pleasure; if he has spent too much time at his desk that should have been spent asleep; if his fine spirits have temporarily become dulled; if he finds the air too damp, the minutes too slow, and the atmosphere too heavy to withstand; if he is obsessed by a fixed idea which bars him from any freedom of thought: if he is any of these poor creatures, we say, let him be given a good pint of amber-flavored chocolate, . . . and marvels will be performed.

—A. Brillat-Savarin, *Physiology of Taste*, 1825

Cakes, Cupcakes,
Panforte, and Pies

• REINE DE SABA •

The first time I came across this recipe was when I was cooking my way, very systematically, through Julia Child's classic *Mastering the Art of French Cooking*. I have made it hundreds of times since, made a few changes, and still consider it to be one of the all-time great chocolate cake recipes. It is a glorious gift to bring to a festive dinner party.

8 ounces semisweet or bittersweet
    chocolate, coarsely chopped
1 cup slivered almonds
3/4 cup plus 3 tablespoons
    granulated sugar
1/2 cup cake flour, sifted before
    measuring
1 1/2 sticks (12 tablespoons)
    unsalted butter, softened to room
    temperature
3 egg yolks, at room temperature

2 tablespoons dark rum
1/2 teaspoon almond extract
3 egg whites, at room temperature
Pinch of salt

Chocolate Ganache Glaze
1 cup heavy cream
10 ounces semisweet or bittersweet
    chocolate, finely chopped
Candied violets for decoration
    (optional)

1. Preheat oven to 350°F. Butter the insides of a 10-inch-round or 8-inch-square cake pan. Line the bottom with parchment paper and butter the paper. Dust with flour and knock out the excess.

2. Melt the chocolate in the top of a double boiler set over (but not touching) barely simmering water. Stir occasionally with a rubber spatula. Remove top of double boiler from heat when most, but not all, of the

chocolate is melted. Stir until all the chocolate is melted and smooth. Set aside to cool.

3. In the bowl of a food processor fitted with a metal blade, pulverize the almonds together with 2 tablespoons of the sugar to make a fine powder. In a small bowl, whisk together the pulverized nuts and the cake flour.

4. In the bowl of an electric mixer, beat the butter and ¾ cup of the sugar together until light and fluffy. Beat in the egg yolks, one at a time, beating well after each addition. Beat in the rum and almond extract. Reduce speed to low and beat in the melted chocolate. Remove bowl from mixer and fold in the almond-flour mixture.

5. In a separate bowl, beat the egg whites and salt until stiff peaks are formed. Sprinkle on the remaining tablespoon of sugar and beat until glossy. Use a rubber spatula to fold the egg whites into the cake mixture in three additions.

6. Pour and scrape the batter into the prepared pan. Bake for 25 to 30 minutes. When done, a cake tester inserted into the cake about 2 inches from the side of the pan should come out clean, but the very center should move slightly if the pan is shaken, and a cake tester should come out covered with wet crumbs.

7. Cool the cake in the pan for 15 minutes, then turn out onto a wire rack to cool completely. If you have baked a square cake, you may cut it into 6 individual servings if you wish. (If you are planning to freeze the cake for future use, freeze it at this point. Bring the cake back to room temperature before frosting.)

8. To make the chocolate ganache glaze, heat the cream in a small saucepan over medium heat until small bubbles begin to appear at the

edges. Remove from the heat and stir in the chocolate, stirring until all the chocolate is melted and the mixture is smooth. Place the wire rack with the cake(s) on it over a sheet of parchment or waxed paper and spread the warm ganache over the top and sides of cake(s). Garnish with candied violets, if desired. Let stand until the glaze is hardened. The cake(s) will keep for several days in the refrigerator.

Yield: 1 10-inch-round cake serving 8 to 10 people, or 6 individual cakes.

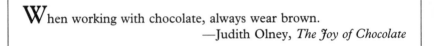

W hen working with chocolate, always wear brown.
—Judith Olney, *The Joy of Chocolate*

Chocolate is loaded with chemical mood enhancers. Almost every component in it has, at some point, been credited with making people feel good. The carbohydrates in chocolate—sugar—trigger the release of serotonin, contributing to the sense of well-being. The sweet taste of the sugar also calms the senses, producing an immediate rush of endorphins. The fat in chocolate enhances flavor and satisfies a primordial urge for more calories. We like the sensations associated with calories coming in, and they come fast with fat.

Then there's phenylethylamine, a chemical that some researchers say stimulates feelings similar to what people experience while in love.
—*Eating Well,* May/June 1995

• CHOCOLATE POUND CAKE •

Chocolate pound cake is an extremely useful item to have on hand throughout the holidays. It keeps well, wrapped in plastic, and you always have a dessert on hand for impromptu entertaining. It is delicious plain or dressed up with ice cream and chocolate sauce. I have cut off wedges and handed them to grateful delivery people. And if I'm very organized I will have a couple in the freezer all wrapped and ready to go.

2 cups unbleached all-purpose
  flour, sifted before measuring
1 cup Dutch process cocoa powder,
  sifted before measuring
½ teaspoon baking powder
½ teaspoon salt
3 sticks (¾ pound) unsalted
  butter, softened to room
  temperature

3 cups granulated sugar
5 large eggs, at room temperature
2 teaspoons vanilla extract
1 cup buttermilk, at room temperature
2 tablespoons instant espresso powder
  dissolved in ¼ cup warm water

1. Preheat oven to 325°F. Generously butter the insides of a 10-inch tube pan, dust with flour, and knock out the excess. (Alternatively, butter and flour two 9 × 5 × 3-inch loaf pans, or three 8 × 4 × 2 ½-inch loaf pans.)

2. In a medium-size bowl, whisk together the flour, cocoa, baking powder, and salt. Set aside.

3. In the bowl of an electric mixer, beat the butter and sugar together at high speed until very light and fluffy. Beat in the eggs, one at a time,

beating briefly after each addition. Beat in the vanilla extract. Reduce speed to low and mix in the flour alternating with buttermilk and dissolved coffee.

4. Pour the batter into the prepared tube pan and bake for 1 hour and 20 minutes (40 to 45 minutes if using smaller loaf pans), or until a cake tester inserted into the center comes out clean.

5. Cool the cake in its pan on a wire rack for 20 minutes. Invert the cake onto a wire rack and let cool completely. Wrapped tightly in plastic wrap, the cake will keep at room temperature for up to 1 week, and for several months in the freezer.

Yield: 1 10-inch cake, or 2 to 3 loaves

Fortunately, chocolate concoctions are still licit in most places. In today's world, when many of yesterday's fashionable habits are today's misdemeanors, we should rejoice that a chocolate dessert can bring so much innocent pleasure, even when a little wickedness is insinuated.
—Marcel Desaulniers, *Death by Chocolate*

• FROSTED CHOCOLATE CUPCAKES •

One of the most popular presents I ever gave was a brand-new cupcake pan filled with these cupcakes and a printed recipe. Kitchen equipment is always a welcome gift, and when it comes with instant gratification it is doubly so. This is the recipe I use.

2 cups cake flour
1/2 cup Dutch process cocoa powder
1 teaspoon baking soda
1/4 teaspoon salt
10 tablespoons unsalted butter,
    softened to room temperature
1 cup granulated sugar
3 large eggs, at room temperature
1 teaspoon vanilla extract

1 cup buttermilk or plain yogurt, at
    room temperature

For the Chocolate Frosting
1/3 cup heavy cream
6 ounces semisweet or bittersweet
    chocolate, coarsely chopped
2 tablespoons unsalted butter, softened
    to room temperature

1. Preheat oven to 350°F. Line 2 cupcake pans with liner paper cups.

2. In a medium-size bowl, whisk together the flour, cocoa powder, baking soda, and salt. Set aside.

3. In the bowl of an electric mixer, beat butter and sugar together until light and fluffy. Beat in the eggs, one at a time, beating well after each addition. Beat in the vanilla. Reduce speed to low and beat in a third of the flour mixture, half of the buttermilk or yogurt, a third of the flour mixture, the rest of the buttermilk or yogurt, and the remaining flour mixture. Beat only until mixture is smooth.

4. Spoon the batter into the cupcake liners, filling only two-thirds full. Bake for 25 minutes, until the tops feel springy to a light touch. Cool cupcakes in their pans for about 10 minutes, then remove them to wire racks to cool completely.

5. To make the frosting, heat the cream in a small saucepan over medium heat until small bubbles begin to appear at the edges. Remove from the heat and stir in the chocolate, stirring until all the chocolate is melted and the mixture is smooth. Stir in the butter until completely melted and smooth. Scrape the mixture into a small bowl and let cool to room temperature.

6. Dip the top of each cupcake into the frosting, then dip each cupcake again until all the frosting has been used. Store in an airtight container at room temperature for 3 to 5 days, or freeze cupcakes for up to 1 month.

Yield: 2 dozen cupcakes

From the court of Montezuma to the court of Spain—so began the odyssey of chocolate, for of all the foods discovered in the new world it was chocolate that underwent the most dramatic transformation. It left its home a bitter stimulant drink and returned as a sweet confection, a food of pleasure, a food of fun.

—Elisabeth Rozin, *Blue Corn and Chocolate*

• CHOCOLATE APPLE CAKE •

Are friends gathering to sing Christmas carols or trim the tree? Fix some hot cider or some Christmas punch and serve with slices of this moist, delicious, spicy chocolate cake.

1½ cups unbleached all-purpose flour, sifted before measuring
6 tablespoons Dutch process cocoa powder
2 teaspoons baking soda
1 teaspoon ground cinnamon
1 teaspoon grated orange zest
¼ teaspoon salt
1½ sticks (12 tablespoons) unsalted butter, softened to room temperature

1¾ cups granulated sugar
3 large eggs, at room temperature
2 cups applesauce
1 cup golden raisins
1 cup broken walnut pieces
Confectioners' sugar to decorate the finished cake

1. Preheat oven to 350°F. Lightly grease the inside of a 10-inch tube pan, line the bottom with parchment paper, and grease the parchment paper. Dust the pan with flour and knock out the excess.

2. In a medium-size bowl, whisk together the flour, cocoa, baking soda, cinnamon, orange zest, and salt.

3. In the bowl of an electric mixer, beat the butter and sugar together at high speed until very light and fluffy. Beat in the eggs, one at a time, until each is completely incorporated. Reduce speed to low and stir in a

third of the flour mixture, followed by half of the applesauce, a third flour mixture, the remaining applesauce, and finally the remaining flour mixture. Beat only long enough to mix in each addition. Fold in the raisins and walnuts with a rubber spatula.

4. Scrape the mixture into the prepared pan, tilting the pan from side to side to distribute the mixture evenly. Bake for 1½ hours, until the cake pulls away from the sides of the pan and the top feels springy to the touch. (The finished cake rises only halfway up the pan.)

5. Cool the cake in the pan on a wire rack for 20 minutes. Invert the cake onto the rack and peel away the parchment paper. Let it cool completely. If not serving immediately, wrap in plastic and store in the refrigerator for up to 1 week. Sift some confectioner's sugar over the cake just before serving.

Yield: 12 to 16 servings

There is, to my mind, no ingredient used in cooking as intensely satisfying and beautifully elegant as chocolate. It imparts a color, flavor, and texture to every recipe in which it is used that proclaim "Here is an important work of art." Its visual properties, its deep luster and gloss are magnificent. A fine chocolate glaze can rival the top of a mahogany Steinway grand piano for beauty.
—Lora Brody, *Growing Up on the Chocolate Diet*

• CHOCOLATE ALMOND PANFORTE •

Panforte, a specialty of Siena, Italy, is a dense, chewy fruitcake-like confection popular during Christmas and New Year's celebrations. Panforte does not always contain chocolate, but this version, which does, is particularly good. It should be made at least 10 days before eating and will keep for several months.

2½ cups whole unblanched
  almonds, toasted
2 cups chopped dried apricots
1 cup chopped dried figs
1 cup golden raisins
2 tablespoons grated orange peel
1 tablespoon grated lemon peel
¾ cup unbleached all-purpose
  flour
¾ cup Dutch process cocoa powder
1½ teaspoons ground cinnamon

1 teaspoon ground coriander
½ teaspoon ground nutmeg
¼ teaspoon ground cloves
¼ teaspoon freshly ground black
  pepper
1 cup granulated sugar
1 cup honey
1 stick (¼ pound) unsalted butter,
  melted
6 ounces bittersweet or semisweet
  chocolate

1. Preheat oven to 300°F. Lightly butter 2 round 8-inch cake pans, line the bottoms with parchment paper, and butter the parchment paper.

2. In a large bowl, combine the almonds, apricots, figs, raisins, and orange and lemon peel.

3. In a smaller bowl, whisk together the flour, cocoa, cinnamon, coriander, nutmeg, cloves, and black pepper. Add to the nut and fruit mixture in the larger bowl and stir to combine.

4. In a heavy medium-size saucepan, combine the sugar, honey, and melted butter. Cook over medium heat, stirring constantly, until the sugar is dissolved. Bring to a boil and continue cooking until a candy thermometer registers 248°F (firm ball stage). Pour over the dry ingredients in the large bowl and mix well with a wooden spoon. (It helps if the spoon has been coated with butter.)

5. Divide the batter between the two prepared pans. Smooth the tops with the back of a wooden spoon. Bake for 1¼ hours, until the tops feel dry to the touch. Cool the cakes in their pans on a wire rack for about 15 minutes. Run a sharp knife around the edges of the pans to loosen the cakes, then turn them out onto the wire rack. Let cool completely.

6. While the cakes are cooling, melt the chocolate in the top of a double boiler set over (but not touching) barely simmering water. Remove from the heat and stir the chocolate until completely smooth.

7. Arrange the cakes, topside up, on plates or cardboard rounds. Spread half the chocolate over each cake and refrigerate until the chocolate is set and hard, about 1 hour.

8. Wrap each cake tightly in plastic wrap and store at room temperature in an airtight container for up to 1 month.

Yield: 2 panforte

✦ CHOCOLATE PECAN PIE ✦

Question: What's the point of eating something as rich and sweet as pecan pie if there is no chocolate in it?

Answer: None. Make a chocolate pecan pie. Then, it's worth the calories.

For the Pie Crust
1½ cups unbleached all-purpose flour
½ teaspoon salt
1 stick (¼ pound) cold unsalted butter, cut into half-inch pieces
4 tablespoons ice water

For the Filling
1½ cups pecans, coarsely chopped
1¼ cups semisweet chocolate chips
1 tablespoon unbleached all-purpose flour
1 stick (¼ pound) unsalted butter, softened to room temperature
½ cup firmly packed dark brown sugar
3 large eggs, at room temperature
¼ teaspoon salt
2 teaspoons vanilla extract
1 tablespoon bourbon
½ cup light corn syrup

1. To make the pie crust, place the flour, salt, and butter in the bowl of a food processor fitted with a metal blade. Pulse, on and off, until the mixture is crumbly. Sprinkle on the water gradually, pulsing, until the dough forms a rough mass. Remove dough from bowl, pat into a disk, wrap in plastic, and refrigerate for 30 minutes.

2. Preheat oven to 350°F.

3. Roll out the dough and tuck it into a 9-inch pie pan. Trim and flute the edges. Reserve leftover dough for a lattice trim if you wish. Prick the bottom of the pie crust with the tines of a fork. Line the dough with foil, fill with dried beans or rice, and bake for 10 minutes. Remove the foil and beans or rice and bake the pie crust for an additional 5 minutes. Remove and set aside while you prepare the filling. Reduce oven temperature to 325°F.

4. In a medium-size bowl, toss together the pecans, chocolate chips, and flour. Set aside.

5. In the bowl of an electric mixer, beat the butter and sugar together until light and fluffy. Beat in the eggs, one at a time, beating well after each addition. Beat in the salt, vanilla, bourbon, and corn syrup. Beat only until mixture is smooth. Remove bowl from electric mixer and stir in the nut mixture.

6. Pour and scrape the filling into the prepared pie shell and bake for 35 to 40 minutes, or until a cake tester inserted into the center comes out clean.

7. Cool completely. The pie will keep for 2 days at room temperature, or for up to 1 month in the freezer.

Yield: 1 9-inch pie

Give us the luxuries of life and we will dispense with the necessities.
—Oliver Wendell Holmes

You can always tell the Christmas season is here when you start getting incredibly dense, tinfoil-and-ribbon-wrapped lumps in the mail. Fruitcakes make ideal gifts because the Postal Service has been unable to find a way to damage them. They last forever, largely because nobody ever eats them. In fact, many smart people save the fruitcakes they receive and send them back to the original givers the next year; some fruitcakes have been passed back and forth for hundreds of years. The easiest way to make a fruitcake is to buy a darkish cake, then pound some old, hard fruit into it with a mallet. Be sure to wear safety glasses.

—Dave Barry, "Simple, Homespun Gifts"

Fancy Breads, Tea Breads, and Coffee Cakes

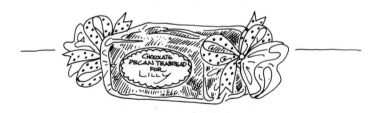

PETITS PAINS AU CHOCOLAT
(LITTLE CHOCOLATE BREADS)

Bread and chocolate, a staple of French schoolchildren, is a heavenly combination. Chocolate-filled croissants are good, but I prefer the simple, straightforward flavor of a crusty hard roll with the surprise of molten chocolate on the inside. These are not at all difficult to make and they live happily in the freezer for a month or so.

½ cup warm milk
2 teaspoons active dry yeast
2 tablespoons honey
2½ cups all-purpose flour, sifted before measuring
3 large eggs, at room temperature

1 teaspoon salt
4 tablespoons unsalted butter, softened to room temperature
4 3-ounce bars finest bittersweet or semisweet chocolate,* each bar divided into 4 equal pieces

1. In the bowl of an electric mixer, combine the milk, yeast, honey, and 2 tablespoons of the flour. Let stand for 15 minutes, until the mixture becomes active and bubbly.

2. On low speed, with paddle attachment, stir in half the remaining flour along with 2 of the eggs and the salt. Increase speed to medium and beat in the butter, 1 tablespoon at a time, until each is completely blended. Lower speed and gradually stir in the remaining flour. Raise the speed to medium and knead for 5 minutes. The dough should feel very smooth but it will remain

*Lindt's Excellence is my favorite for this recipe.

sticky. Remove to a lightly floured surface and knead by hand for a few minutes. Wash, dry, and butter the insides of the bowl. Return the dough to the bowl, cover with plastic wrap, and refrigerate for 4 hours or overnight.

3. Preheat oven to 350°F. Line two large baking sheets with parchment paper.

4. Remove the dough to a lightly floured surface. Knead lightly and divide the dough in half. Divide each piece in half and continue until you have 16 pieces of dough. Roll each piece of dough into a square or rectangle. Place a piece of chocolate in the center and fold the dough around it to enclose completely. Pinch dough together to seal. Arrange the chocolate breads 1 inch apart on the prepared baking sheets, cover with a clean towel, and let rise for 1 hour.

5. Preheat oven to 350°F. Beat the remaining egg and brush the tops of the breads. Bake for 20 minutes, until the breads are golden brown. Remove to wire racks to cool. If the rolls are not to be eaten the same day, they can be frozen for up to 1 month. Defrost at room temperature inside their plastic bag, then pop them into a 325°F oven for 5 to 10 minutes.

Yield: 16 petits pains

The craving for chocolate is sensory. It's a desire for the oral experience of chocolate: the odor, the smoothness, the flavor.
                    —Paul Rozin, quoted in *Eating Well,* May/June 1995

• CHOCOLATE COFFEE CAKE •

If you're planning a holiday brunch or an afternoon gathering, this yeasty, rich, coffee cake filled with nuts and chocolate is the thing to serve. Set the dough to rise in the refrigerator overnight and bake it fresh the following day. Or bake it way ahead and store it in the freezer.

1 cup whole milk, warmed
1 tablespoon active dry yeast
¼ cup honey, plus an additional
  ¼ to ½ cup
5 cups unbleached all-purpose
  flour, sifted before measuring
3 large eggs, at room temperature
1 teaspoon salt
1 stick (¼ pound) unsalted butter,
  softened to room temperature
3 ounces bittersweet or semisweet
  chocolate, grated

½ cup toasted walnuts, finely chopped
½ cup toasted almonds, finely
  chopped
½ cup toasted hazelnuts, finely
  chopped
½ cup granulated sugar
1 teaspoon ground cinnamon
4 tablespoons unsalted butter, melted
  and cooled

1. Butter the insides of a 9-inch springform pan and line the bottom with parchment paper. Set aside.

2. In the bowl of an electric mixer, combine the milk, yeast, ¼ cup honey, and 2 tablespoons of the flour. Let stand for 15 minutes, until the mixture becomes active and bubbly.

3. On low speed, with paddle attachment, stir in half the remaining flour

along with 2 of the eggs and the salt. Increase speed to medium and beat in the softened butter, 2 tablespoons at a time, until each addition is completely blended. Lower speed and gradually stir in the remaining flour. Raise the speed to medium and knead for 5 minutes. The dough should feel very smooth but it will remain sticky. Remove to a lightly floured surface and knead by hand for a few minutes. Wash, dry, and butter the insides of the bowl. Return the dough to the bowl, cover with plastic wrap, and refrigerate for 4 hours or overnight.

4. In a medium-size bowl, combine the grated chocolate, chopped nuts, sugar, cinnamon, and melted butter to make a paste.

5. Remove the dough to a lightly floured surface and knead it briefly. Cut off about a quarter of the dough and roll it out into a large circle, about 14 inches in diameter. Stretch the dough circle to fit into the prepared pan, crimping the top edges to resemble a pie shell. Spread a quarter of the chocolate-nut mixture on the bottom of the dough shell.

6. Roll out the remaining dough into a rectangle measuring about 8 by 12 inches. Spread the remaining chocolate mixture over the rectangle, leaving about 1 inch along all the edges. Roll up the rectangle starting with the long side, then cut the roll into 1-inch segments. Place these inside the dough shell, cut side up. Cover with a clean towel and let rise for 1 hour. (Or place in refrigerator overnight.)

7. Preheat oven to 350°F. Beat the remaining egg and brush over the top of the coffee cake. Bake for 45 minutes, until top is golden brown. Let cool in pan on a wire rack.

Yield: 8 to 10 servings

• CHOCOLATE GINGERBREAD •

I love gingerbread any time, but I find this sweet, spicy cake particularly welcome during the holiday season. As you can imagine, an infusion of chocolate makes an already good thing very much better. Packed in a pretty tin, gingerbread makes a great gift for mailing to faraway friends and family.

3 ounces bittersweet or semisweet chocolate, coarsely chopped
½ cup Lyle's Golden Syrup or honey
½ cup canola oil
4 tablespoons unsalted butter
2½ cups unbleached all-purpose flour, sifted before measuring
⅔ cup firmly packed light brown sugar
1 teaspoon baking soda
1 teaspoon baking powder

1 teaspoon ground ginger
¼ teaspoon ground cinnamon
¼ teaspoon freshly grated nutmeg
¼ teaspoon salt
2 large eggs, at room temperature
1 teaspoon vanilla extract
Small knob of fresh ginger (about 1 inch), peeled and grated
1 cup buttermilk, at room temperature
⅔ cup semisweet mini chocolate chips
Confectioners' sugar for decorating

1. Preheat oven to 350°F. Lightly grease the bottom and sides of a 9-inch springform pan. Line bottom with parchment paper.

2. Melt the chocolate together with Lyle's Golden Syrup, canola oil, and butter in the top of a double boiler set over (but not touching) barely simmering water. Remove from the heat, stir until smooth, and set aside.

3. In a large bowl, whisk together the flour, brown sugar, baking soda,

baking powder, ground ginger, cinnamon, nutmeg, and salt. In a smaller bowl, whisk the eggs until they are foamy, then whisk in the vanilla, grated ginger, and buttermilk.

4. Make a well in the center of the flour mixture and pour in the buttermilk mixture. Stir with a wooden spoon to combine. Beat in the chocolate mixture with an electric mixer or a wooden spoon, until well combined. Stir in the chocolate chips.

5. Pour into prepared pan and bake for 35 to 40 minutes, until a tester inserted into the center comes out clean. Let cool in pan for 10 to 15 minutes, then remove cake from the pan and dust with confectioners' sugar before serving. The gingerbread is delicious warm from the oven or allowed to mellow for a few days. It will keep, wrapped in plastic, for 1 week.

Yield: 1 chocolate gingerbread

Research tells us that fourteen out of any ten individuals like chocolate.

—Sandra Boynton, *Chocolate: The Consuming Passion*

◆ CHOCOLATE CRANBERRY TEA BREAD ◆

This tea bread is quick and easy to prepare and makes a wonderful gift. It can be made as one large loaf or four mini loaves. It will keep, tightly wrapped, for up to a week and for months in the freezer. It needs only to be thawed to room temperature before it becomes deliciously edible once more. But I remember one evening when I wanted something good to nibble on, I pulled a loaf out of the freezer and cut thin slices from the frozen loaf—they were so good.

2 ounces bittersweet or semisweet chocolate, coarsely chopped
1¼ cups unbleached all-purpose flour
1 teaspoon baking powder
½ teaspoon ground cinnamon
¼ teaspoon salt
1 stick (¼ pound) unsalted butter, softened to room temperature

⅓ cup firmly packed light brown sugar
⅓ cup granulated sugar
3 large eggs, at room temperature
1 teaspoon vanilla extract
½ cup dried cranberries
½ cup finely chopped whole almonds

1. Preheat oven to 350°F. Butter the bottom and sides of a 9 × 5 × 3-inch loaf pan (or four 5½ × 3 × 2½-inch mini pans) and line the bottom(s) with parchment paper. Set aside.

2. Melt the chocolate in the top of a double boiler set over (but not touching) barely simmering water. Remove from the heat and set aside to cool slightly.

3. In a medium-size bowl, whisk together the flour, baking powder, cinnamon, and salt.

4. In the bowl of an electric mixer, cream the butter and both sugars together until very light and fluffy. Beat in the eggs, one at a time, followed by the vanilla extract and the melted chocolate. Reduce speed and stir in the flour mixture, the cranberries, and the almonds.

5. Scrape the mixture into the prepared pan(s) and bake for 45 to 50 minutes in the large pan and about 30 minutes in the mini loaf pans, until a cake tester inserted into the center comes out clean.

6. Remove the pan(s) from the oven and let cool for 15 minutes. Turn the bread out of the pan onto a wire rack and allow to cool completely.

Yield: 1 large loaf or 4 mini loaves

WHAT ABOUT CAFFEINE?

There are 5 to 10 milligrams of caffeine in one ounce of bittersweet chocolate, 5 milligrams in an ounce of milk chocolate, and 10 milligrams in a six-ounce cup of cocoa; by contrast, there are 100 to 150 milligrams of caffeine in an eight-ounce cup of brewed coffee. You would have to eat more than a dozen Hershey bars, for example, to get the amount of caffeine in one cup of coffee.

• CHOCOLATE PECAN TEA BREAD •

Another quick and easy tea bread to make for your own entertaining or to give away during the holidays.

1¼ cups unbleached all-purpose
   flour
⅓ cup cake flour
1 teaspoon baking powder
¼ teaspoon salt
1 stick (¼ pound) unsalted butter,
   softened to room temperature
½ cup granulated sugar

½ cup firmly packed light brown
   sugar
2 large eggs, at room temperature
1 teaspoon vanilla extract
⅔ cup milk, at room temperature
¾ cup broken pecan pieces
1½ cups bittersweet or semisweet
   chocolate chips

1. Preheat oven to 350°F. Butter the bottom and sides of a 9 × 5 × 3-inch loaf pan (or four 5½ × 3 × 2½-inch mini pans). Dust with flour and knock out any excess. Set aside.

2. In a medium-size bowl whisk together the flours, baking powder, and salt.

3. In the bowl of an electric mixer, beat the butter and granulated sugar together until light and fluffy. Beat in the light brown sugar and continue to beat until completely incorporated. Beat in the eggs, one at a time, until well mixed, then beat in the vanilla extract.

4. Reduce speed to low and stir in half of the flour mixture, followed by the milk, then the rest of the flour mixture. Stir in the pecan pieces and the chocolate chips.

5. Scrape the mixture into the prepared pan(s) and bake for 45 to 50 minutes in the large pan and about 30 minutes in the mini loaf pans, until a skewer inserted into the center comes out clean.

6. Cool the bread(s) in the pan(s) on a wire rack for 10 minutes. Remove the bread(s) and cool on the wire rack. Wrap tightly in plastic wrap and store in an airtight container at room temperature for up to 1 week, or freeze for up to 1 month.

Yield: 1 large loaf or 4 mini loaves

I stopped believing in Santa Claus when I was six. Mother took me to see him in a department store and he asked for my autograph.
—Shirley Temple Black, actress, singer, and United States ambassador

• CHOCOLATE RAISIN KUGELHOPF •

The kugelhopf is a yeast cake that originated in Austria, birthplace of so many great cakes and pastries. It is said that Carême, the great French pastry cook, was given the recipe by the chef of the Austrian ambassador and that Marie Antoinette was very fond of it. And I predict that you, too, will be very fond of it, once you have tasted this chocolate-flecked version.

1 cup whole milk
1 stick (¼ pound) unsalted butter
½ cup granulated sugar
1 teaspoon vanilla extract
½ teaspoon salt
4½ cups unbleached all-purpose
   flour
1 package active dry yeast

3 large eggs, at room temperature
¼ cup light brown sugar
1 cup golden raisins
5 ounces bittersweet or semisweet
   chocolate, finely chopped
2 tablespoons unsalted butter, melted
Confectioners' sugar for decorating

1. Heavily coat the insides of a 9-inch kugelhopf mold or a 10-inch tube pan with butter. Set aside.

2. In a medium-size saucepan, scald the milk and remove from heat. Stir in the butter, sugar, vanilla extract, and salt. When the butter has melted, transfer the milk to the bowl of a heavy-duty electric mixer and let cool to lukewarm. Use the paddle attachment, on low speed, to stir in 1½ cups of the flour and the yeast. Stir in the eggs and the remaining 3 cups of flour, adding it ½ cup at a time. Beat at medium speed until the dough starts to come away from the sides of the bowl.

3. Remove the dough to a lightly floured surface and knead briefly until the dough feels smooth and satiny. Wash, dry, and lightly butter the bowl and replace the dough. Let it rise in a warm place, covered loosely with a kitchen towel, for 1 to 1½ hours, until doubled in bulk.

4. While the dough is rising, prepare the filling. In a small bowl combine the sugar, raisins, and chocolate. Set aside.

5. When the dough has risen, punch it down, remove it to a lightly floured surface, and knead briefly. Let it rest for 5 minutes, then roll it out into a rectangle (about 12 by 24 inches). Spread the melted butter over the dough and sprinkle with the chocolate-raisin mixture, leaving a 1-inch border all around. Starting with the long side, roll up the dough tightly, stretching it out a little bit. With a sharp knife, cut the roll into 12 even slices. Arrange 6 slices lining the sides of the pan, then arrange the remaining 6 slices inside the outer layer of slices. Cut sides should be facing each other. Cover loosely with a kitchen towel and let it stand in a warm place until the dough reaches the top of the pan, about 1 hour.

6. Preheat oven to 350°F.

7. Bake the kugelhopf for 45 minutes to 1 hour, until a cake tester inserted into the center comes out clean. Remove from oven and turn out of the pan onto a wire rack. Let cool completely. If you are not serving it the same day, wrap well in plastic wrap or foil and freeze for up to 3 months. Dust with confectioners' sugar before serving.

Yield: 1 kugelhopf

Sweets for
the Sweet

• CHOCOLATE TRUFFLE SQUARES •

Almonds and cinnamon enhance the flavor of these truffles, which are made in a pan and cut into squares. These are the truffles to prepare if you don't want to mess around with rolling chocolate ganache into balls.

16 ounces bittersweet chocolate
½ cup heavy cream
¼ cup amaretto
¼ teaspoon ground cinnamon

⅓ cup toasted almonds, coarsely
  chopped
Foil or paper petit four cups

1. Line the bottom of an 8-inch-square baking pan with parchment paper.

2. Using a chef's knife, chop 12 ounces of the chocolate very fine.

3. In a small saucepan, heat the cream over medium heat until small bubbles begin to appear at the edges. Remove from the heat and stir in the finely chopped chocolate, stirring until all the chocolate is melted and the mixture is smooth. Whisk in the amaretto and cinnamon. Set aside to cool.

4. Melt the remaining 4 ounces of chocolate in the top of a double boiler set over (but not touching) barely simmering water. Remove top of double boiler from heat and pour half of the melted chocolate into the prepared pan. Tilt the pan to spread the chocolate in an even layer across the bottom. Refrigerate the pan for 5 minutes to harden the chocolate.

5. Spread the ganache mixture over the hardened chocolate, then drizzle the remaining melted chocolate all over the ganache and spread it lightly with a rubber spatula. Sprinkle the almonds over the top and press them

lightly into the melted chocolate. Refrigerate for 3 to 4 hours, until very firm. Turn out onto a cutting board and peel away the parchment paper. Use a long, sharp knife to cut into 1-inch squares. Place the chocolate squares into foil or paper petit four cups and store them in an airtight container in the refrigerator for up to 2 weeks.

Yield: 64 chocolate truffle squares

I had a mind to be friends again with chocolate, and so took some the day before yesterday, by way of digesting my dinner, that I might make the better supper: and yesterday took some again by way of nourishment, to enable me to fast till supper-time: it had every way the desired effect: and what I think very extraordinary is, that it acted according to my wishes.
        —Mme de Sévigné, just 6 months later, October 28, 1671

• CHOCOLATE HAZELNUT TRUFFLES •

Homemade chocolate truffles always make an impression out of all proportion to how easy they are to make. Serve them at the end of an elegant dinner party or pack them in a confectionery box and give them to a very deserving person.

1¼ cups heavy cream
12 ounces semisweet or bittersweet
   chocolate, coarsely chopped
¼ cup Dutch process cocoa powder

1 cup toasted hazelnuts, finely
   chopped
Foil or paper petit four cups
   (optional)

1. In a small heavy saucepan, scald the cream over medium heat. Remove from heat.

2. Break up the chocolate and process it in a food processor with a steel blade until the particles are very small. With the motor running, pour in the hot cream through the funnel and process until the chocolate is melted and mixture is very smooth. Pour into a bowl, cover with plastic wrap, and refrigerate for 3 to 4 hours, until mixture is cold and almost hard.

3. Spread a large sheet of waxed paper on your work surface. Pour the chopped hazelnuts in one pile and the cocoa in another. Scoop a rounded teaspoonful of the chocolate mixture into your hand. Roll into a ball approximately 1 inch in diameter. Roll chocolate ball in hazelnuts, pressing nuts into the chocolate, then roll in cocoa. Place each ball inside a petit four cup or place them in a plastic airtight container. These will keep for 1 week in the refrigerator. Let the truffles stand at room temperature before serving.

Yield: 4 dozen truffles

The first Hershey bar was produced in 1894, and Hershey's Kisses began rolling off the line in 1907. These inexpensive, highly sweetened milk-enriched confections were an instant success and the chocolate candy bar became the right of every American, rich or poor.

—Elisabeth Rozin, *Blue Corn and Chocolate*

• CHOCOLATE BOURBON TRUFFLES •

You can vary these slightly alcoholic truffles by substituting rum, Cognac, kirsch, Grand Marnier, Sambuca, or grappa for the bourbon. Although the alcohol imparts a very definite flavor, 3 tablespoons of liquor divided among 3 dozen truffles does not make the truffles very lethal.

8 ounces semisweet or bittersweet
chocolate, coarsely chopped
1 stick (¼ pound) unsalted butter
⅔ cup finely chopped toasted
almonds

3 tablespoons bourbon
½ cup Dutch process cocoa powder
½ cup confectioners' sugar

1. Melt the chocolate and butter in the top of a double boiler set over (but not touching) barely simmering water. Remove from the heat and stir until smooth. Stir in the almonds and the bourbon. Pour into a small bowl, cover, and refrigerate until firm, about 1 hour.

2. In a medium-size bowl, whisk together the cocoa and confectioners' sugar.

3. Scoop a rounded teaspoonful of the chocolate mixture into your hand. Working quickly, roll each truffle between the palms of your hands into a smooth ball. Roll each ball in the cocoa mixture to coat. Store the truffles in an airtight container in the refrigerator for up to 1 week. Let stand for 15 minutes at room temperature before serving.

Yield: about 3 dozen truffles

I came to know chocolate as a distinct personality, with almost as many foibles and traits as any living creature. (If, for instance, chocolate has a gender, I am convinced it must be feminine, for certainly it demands to be treated and handled with all the respect due a temperamental *grande dame*.)

—Judith Olney, *The Joy of Chocolate*

• CHOCOLATE ALMOND MOUNDS •

Another easy-to-make chocolate confection flavored with toasted almonds and caramelized sugar.

1 cup blanched, slivered almonds
1 tablespoon granulated sugar
8 ounces semisweet or bittersweet
  chocolate, coarsely chopped

2 tablespoons unsalted butter, softened
  to room temperature
Foil or paper petit four cups

1. Preheat oven to 350°F.
2. Spread the almonds on a jelly roll pan and sprinkle them with the sugar. Bake for 15 to 20 minutes, until the sugar has melted and the almonds turn a light golden brown. Watch them carefully and shake the pan from time to time to brown the almonds evenly. Remove from the oven and set aside.
3. Melt the chocolate in the top of a double boiler set over (but not touching) barely simmering water. Remove from the heat and stir in the butter until the mixture is very smooth.
4. Add the almonds and stir until the nuts are evenly distributed.
5. Drop teaspoonfuls of the mixture into foil or paper petit four cups and let stand at room temperature until completely cool and hard. Store in an airtight container at room temperature, for several weeks.

Yield: about 18 mounds

• CHOCOLATE RAISIN-PEANUT CLUSTERS •

These old-fashioned candies couldn't be quicker or easier to make. I like to pack them in small boxes to slip into Christmas stockings. And I know many a late-night Santa who wouldn't mind finding a small plate of these left out for him.

*8 ounces semisweet or bittersweet
    chocolate
½ cup raisins*

*½ cup unsalted shelled peanuts
Foil or paper petit four cups*

1. Melt the chocolate in the top of a double boiler set over (but not touching) barely simmering water. Remove top of double boiler from the heat and set aside to cool slightly.

2. Stir in the raisins and peanuts. Scoop a small spoonful of the mixture and use another spoon to drop it into foil or paper petit four cups. Chill in the refrigerator until set.

Yield: 1 pound

• CHOCOLATE-DIPPED STRAWBERRIES •

Without question, strawberries are a luxury in December, and a box of hand-dipped, chocolate-covered strawberries makes a luxurious and memorable gift. Look for long-stem Driscoll strawberries, which start to appear this time of year. These are grown especially for fondues and dipping, and are exceptionally clean so they don't need to be washed.

12 to 16 large, long-stem
strawberries or
20 smaller strawberries with leaves

6 ounces semisweet or bittersweet
chocolate, coarsely chopped

1. Line a tray or baking sheet with waxed paper or parchment paper.

2. Look over the strawberries and rinse them gently, if necessary. Pat dry with paper towels. Lay them out on more paper towels and let dry completely. The chocolate won't adhere if the strawberries are damp.

3. Melt the chocolate in the top of a double boiler set over (but not touching) barely simmering water. Stir the mixture occasionally with a rubber spatula. Remove top of double boiler from heat when most, but not all of the chocolate is melted. Stir until all the chocolate is melted and smooth. Let cool until tepid.

4. Dip the pointed end of each strawberry in the melted chocolate so that half the berry is covered. Let excess chocolate drip away and place the berry on prepared tray.

5. When all the berries have been dipped, refrigerate them for about 15 minutes, until the chocolate hardens. Arrange them on crumpled

tissue paper in an airtight plastic container and refrigerate for up to 4 or 5 days.

Yield: 12 to 16 chocolate-dipped strawberries

Double-Dipped Strawberries

To make extra-luxurious double-dipped strawberries, prepare strawberries and line trays with waxed paper as described above. Melt 5 ounces coarsely chopped white chocolate as described above. Dip the strawberries and cool in refrigerator. Melt the dark chocolate, dip strawberries to cover the white chocolate, following procedure described above.

• CHOCOLATE-DIPPED APRICOTS •

Search out the juiciest, plumpest glacéed apricots you can find to make these chocolate-covered, nut-encrusted beauties. You can prepare these weeks before you will need them. Arrange them in a pretty tin or plain paper candy boxes and send or bring them to a lucky recipient.

6 ounces semisweet or bittersweet chocolate, coarsely chopped
16 to 20 glacéed apricots

½ cup finely chopped pistachios or walnuts

1. Line a tray or baking sheet with waxed paper or parchment paper.
2. Melt the chocolate in the top of a double boiler set over (but not touching) barely simmering water. Stir the mixture occasionally with a rubber spatula. Remove top of double boiler from heat when most, but not all, of the chocolate is melted. Stir until all the chocolate is melted and smooth. Let cool until tepid.
3. Dip each apricot halfway into the chocolate, let excess chocolate drip away, and dip the tip of the chocolate-covered apricot into the finely chopped nuts. Arrange the dipped apricots on the prepared tray.
4. Refrigerate the apricots for about 15 minutes, until the chocolate hardens. Arrange them on crumpled tissue paper in an airtight plastic container and store at room temperature. They will keep for several months.

Yield: 16 to 20 chocolate-dipped apricots

You never have to figure out what to get for children, because they'll tell you exactly what they want. They spend months and months researching these kinds of things by watching Saturday-morning cartoon-show advertisements. Make sure you get your children exactly what they ask for, even if you disapprove of their choices. If your child thinks he wants Murderous Bob, the Doll with the Face You Can Rip Right Off, you'd better get it. You may be worried that it might help to encourage your child's antisocial tendencies, but believe me, you have not seen antisocial tendencies until you've seen a child who is convinced that he or she did not get the right gift.

—Dave Barry, "Christmas Shopping: A Survivor's Guide"

◆ HOT FUDGE SAUCE ◆

A pretty jar of Hot Fudge Sauce is a luxurious and indulgent gift. Accompany it with a small card telling your lucky recipient that the sauce should be refrigerated; can be eaten as a spread when it is cold; or can be warmed by placing the jar in a pan of hot water. When it is hot it can be spooned over ice cream, cake, or brownies. A jar of homemade Hot Fudge Sauce is a jar of pure pleasure!

2 cups heavy cream
½ cup firmly packed brown sugar
8 ounces semisweet or bittersweet chocolate, finely chopped

2 tablespoons unsweetened chocolate, finely chopped
2 tablespoons unsalted butter
1 tablespoon vanilla extract

1. In a large saucepan, bring the cream to a boil, reduce heat to a simmer, and cook, stirring occasionally, until the cream is reduced by half, about 20 minutes.

2. Stir in the sugar and cook, stirring, until the sugar has dissolved.

3. Remove from heat and stir in both chocolates and the butter. Keep stirring until all the chocolate is melted and very smooth. Stir in the vanilla extract. Let cool to room temperature and pour into small, pretty jars. The sauce will keep in the refrigerator for up to 1 month.

Yield: about 3 cups

Always serve too much hot fudge sauce on hot fudge sundaes. It makes people overjoyed, and puts them in your debt.

—Judith Olney, *The Joy of Chocolate*

How to Pack
and Ship

- Make the wrapping as important as the gift. Collect baskets, tins, boxes, ribbons, and wrappings all year, especially at yard sales, bazaars, flea markets, craft sales, and antiques shops.
- For a gift to a fellow baker, include a special utensil: beautiful copper cookie cutters; a nutmeg grater with a supply of whole nutmeg; a kugelhopf pan, or even a set of heavy-duty wire cooling racks.
- Select the right container. Cookie tins, sturdy boxes with lids such as hat boxes, and plastic containers with tight-fitting lids are all excellent containers for shipping baked goods. Keep in mind that the container becomes part of the gift, so match the container to the person. A special friend might love a flowered hat box, while a more practical one would be very happy with a large, reusable plastic container. (Somehow no kitchen ever has enough of these.) In a pinch, a sturdy cardboard box, such as are sold at post offices, will do very well.
- Tissue paper and waxed paper are your friends. Tissue paper provides insulation as well as a festive look. Insulate your container with several layers of tissue paper on the bottom and top and layer waxed paper between each layer of cookies, biscotti, or brownies. Close the container and use tape to secure the lid. Additional gift wrapping is up to you.
- Mailing cartons and packing material. The mailing carton should be made of heavy cardboard and be substantially larger than your gift package so that there is room for packing material to insulate the cake, bread, or cookies from the harsh outside world. There are lots of excellent packing materials around: crumpled-up newspaper is cheap and easy to come by; crumpled tissue paper is fine; popped (unbuttered) popcorn is excellent and biodegradable; styrofoam peanuts and bubble

wrap are very effective, if ecologically unsound. Whatever you use, there should be several inches of packing material between all sides of the mailing carton and the package inside.

GIFTS DELIVERED BY HAND

Baked gifts that you will be delivering by hand, either as Christmas gifts, contributions to an evening's entertainment, or as gifts for your dinner host or hostess, can be packaged in a great variety of ways. Here are some ideas:

- decorative cookie tins
- antique cookie jars
- large, wide-mouth glass jars with cork stoppers
- decorative plates and platters wrapped with colored cellophane
- Chinese food take-out containers lined with colored tissue paper
- pretty hat boxes lined with tissue paper
- woven baskets lined with tissue paper and wrapped with cellophane
- mylar bags such as are used for liquor bottles are good for wrapping biscotti and cookies

Some Notes on
Equipment

Electric mixer: Many recipes in this book call for a heavy-duty electric mixer. I find mine indispensable for mixing and kneading dough, creaming butter, and beating eggs.

Food processor: Some recipes call for the use of a food processor. It is used to chop nuts and to cut butter into dry ingredients.

Saucepan and double boiler: A heavyweight saucepan is needed to reduce syrups and a double boiler is necessary for melting chocolate. If these are coated with a nonstick surface, all the better when it comes to cleaning up.

Measuring cups: You should have two kinds—a set of metal or plastic nesting cups with flat rims for dry ingredients and glass measuring cups with a pouring spout and clear markings, for liquid ingredients.

Measuring spoons: It is useful to have at least two sets of standard, graduated measuring spoons.

Mixing bowls: Have an assortment of large, medium, and small mixing bowls.

Wire whisk: Whisks are useful for blending flour with other dry ingredients, but if you don't have one you can use a fork.

Wooden spoons and rubber spatulas: Wooden spoons are used for hand mixing and rubber spatulas for folding ingredients into a batter.

Rolling pin: A sturdy rolling pin is essential and it is wise to invest in a heavy, hardwood rolling pin with ball bearings.

Cookie sheets: Use heavyweight, shiny, metal cookie sheets. Avoid dark-colored baking sheets. Edges should be flat or barely turned up, so that heat can reach cookies evenly from all directions. Insulated baking sheets are fine, but they will require a slightly longer baking time, usually the maximum baking time given in the recipe. Nonstick baking sheets, if they are made of heavyweight metal and coated with a top-quality nonstick material, are also good. (If any of your baking sheets are light and flimsy, do yourself a favor and throw them out.) If you are short of cookie sheets and want to use a jelly roll pan, turn it upside down and use that side. Otherwise, the raised edges will impede the flow of air to the cookies.

Baking pans. Other than cookie sheets, you will need to have on hand the following baking pans:

- Standard metal loaf pans measuring 9 × 5 × 3 inches, and miniature loaf pans measuring 5 × 3 × 2⅛ inches.
- Square and rectangular baking pans measuring 9 × 9 × 2 inches and 8 × 8 × 2 inches and 13 × 9 × 2 inches
- Two 8-inch-round cake pans
- A 9-inch springform pan
- A 9-inch kugelhopf mold
- A 10-inch tube pan
- Cupcake pans

Baking parchment: An indispensable aid in my kitchen. It eliminates the need to grease cookie sheets or to ever clean them again. I dislike the parchment in rolls and buy it in sheets from Maid of Scandinavia or The King Arthur Flour Baker's Catalogue (see sources, page 123). I find that I can use a sheet of parchment two or three times before discarding it. Aluminum foil (shiny side out) can be used instead of baking parchment in many recipes.

Oven thermometer: I've never found an oven that wasn't several degrees off, and an oven thermometer makes it possible for you to adjust the difference. Put the thermometer in the center of the oven when you turn it on. Wait 15 minutes to check the temperature and make the necessary adjustment. If the discrepancy is more than 50°F, you should have your oven calibrated.

Timer: The only time I have ever burned entire batches of cookies was when I tried to do it without a timer. Set your timer to go off in the minimum baking time, so you can check the cookies.

Wire cooling racks: Raised wire racks allow baked goods to cool quickly because the air reaches them from all directions.

Spatulas: You will find it useful to have several different kinds of spatulas. A narrow metal spatula is used for leveling off dry ingredients and for loosening the edges of cookies or brownies from a pan. A wide, flexible metal spatula is used to remove baked cookies or biscotti from the baking sheets to a cooling rack. Rubber spatulas are used to scrape down the sides of a mixing bowl.

Strainers: Use a large metal strainer to strain confectioners' sugar and brown sugar to remove any lumps. Use a small, fine-meshed strainer for sifting confectioners' sugar over baked cakes, breads, and cookies and for straining lemon juice.

Plastic wrap: Very handy for wrapping up doughs that need refrigeration before rolling out.

Storage containers and plastic food storage bags: These fall into two categories. Very useful and ugly. Pretty but useless for long-term storage. For storage at home I use the former—plastic containers with very tight-fitting lids. For gift wrapping and mailing I collect tins, boxes, baskets, etc.

Mail-Order Sources

The King Arthur Flour Baker's Catalogue
P.O. Box 876
Norwich, Vermont 05055
(800) 827–6836
Merckens chocolate, chips, and cocoa. Van Leer chocolate and cocoa. Excellent variety of flours (many stone-ground and organic), flavorings and spices, Boyajian citrus oils, parchment paper in sheets.

Maid of Scandinavia
32–44 Raleigh Avenue
Minneapolis, Minnesota 55416
(800) 328–6722
Candy boxes, cookie, pie, and cake boxes, doilies, moisture-resistant poly wrap, and a wide variety of gift-wrapping supplies. Special pans, baking equipment, cookie cutters, decorating equipment.

Walnut Acres
Penns Creek, Pennsylvania 17862
(717) 837–3874
Large selection of flours and grains; very good selection of dried fruits (many organic) and nuts.

Williams-Sonoma
Mail-Order Department
P.O. Box 7456
San Francisco, California 94120–7456
(415) 421–4242
Callebaut chocolate, special pans, cookie sheets, etc.

Index